D1553424

WHITE
NOISE

THE
EMINEM COLLECTION

Edited by

HILTON ALS and
DARRYL A. TURNER

DEER PARK PUBLIC LIBRARY
44 LAKE AVENUE
DEER PARK, NY 11729

Thunder's Mouth Press • New York

WHITE NOISE

Compilation copyright © 2003 by Hilton Als

Published by
Thunder's Mouth Press
An Imprint of Avalon Publishing Group Incorporated
245 W. 17th St., 11th Floor
New York, NY 10011

All rights reserved. No part of this book may be
reproduced or transmitted in any form without
written permission from the publisher, except by
reviewers who may quote brief excerpts
in connection with a review.

Library of Congress Cataloging-in-Publication Data:

White Noise : the Eminem collection /
edited by Hilton Als with Darryl A. Turner
p.cm.
ISBN 1-56025-534-X
1. Eminem (Musician)
2. Rap musicians–United States–Biography.
3. Rap musicians–United States–Interviews.
I. Als, Hilton. II. Turner, Darryl A.

ML420.E56W45   2003
782.421649'092–dc22

2003061642

9 8 7 6 5 4 3 2 1

Designed by Pauline Neuwirth, Neuwirth & Associates, Inc..

Printed in the United States of America
Distributed by Publishers Group West

contents

DEER PARK PUBLIC LIBRARY
44 LAKE AVENUE
DEER PARK, NY 11729

CONTENTS

NOISE

there's a certain redundancy of tone to many, if not most, of the public discussions that Marshall Mathers III has engendered in his by now thirteen-year career as the recording artist and producer generally known as Eminem. On one side stand Mathers' apologists—rock critics, academics, "wiggers" and the like—who cite the rapper as an officer in the war against at least one political fiction: "Liberty and Justice for all, now and forever." As a way of explaining his "rage," Mathers' supporters turn to his biography. They describe him as a lower class id joyfully eviscerating Mom, faggots, Viocodin, and everything else Americans hold dear—or love to hate—because America could never hold him or anyone like him dearly.

It's outrageous, this white boy not a white boy. This nasal sounding harridan hurling words at Church and State backed by a 4/4 beat? "Fuck you Ms. Cheney/Fuck you Tipper Gore/ Fuck you with the freest speech this divided states of embarrassment will allow me to have," he declares in "White America," one of nineteen tracks on his 2002 release, *The Eminem Show*. What can be done with this trickster whose

phallus is made limp by a nation whose standards of beauty—
"Britney's garbage/What's this bitch retarded? Gimme back
my sixteen dollars"—are as ridiculous to him as the popular
custodians of his country's musical culture, who cast a wary
eye on his mouth, his mind, his body. "I ain't Back Street and
Ricky Martin," he opines on "Marshall Mathers," one of eighteen tracks making up his 2000 release, *The Marshall Mathers
LP*, "With instincts to kill N'Sync, don't get me started."

Born in St. Joseph, Missouri, in 1973, Mathers' mother,
Debbie Mathers-Briggs, has described giving birth to her eld-
est child as a "living hell." And mother certainly gave birth to
the son when it comes to language. Mrs. Mathers-Briggs (the
second marriage would end in divorce, too) was barely out of
her teens when she separated from Mathers' father. Thus
unencumbered, she hit the road with her young son in tow,
staying first with relatives in various parts of the Midwest—
North Dakota, Missouri—before making a provisional home
for herself and her boy in Warren, Michigan.

Warren: a blue-collar suburb of Detroit populated by white
laborers from the South who so longed for the "old country"
and the old ways that they referred to their small community
as "Warren-tucky." Confederate flags in the window, beer for
breakfast, and watery hominy grits ladled onto chipped enam-
el plates by women whose time was split between being a wait-
ress and Mom, if there is a distinction to be made.

In any case, as Marshall was growing up, the ghosts and
artifacts of the "old country" were everywhere, especially its
language, "the enduring speech of *ain'ts* and *hain'ts* and *hits
down yonder*, elevated by friendly philologists to an honorable
heritage from old England or Scotland," as Elizabeth Hardwick tells us, in an essay about the legendary Seabiscuit,
recalling the sound of the conversation she overheard while
growing up in Lexington, Kentucky, in the nineteen-thirties
and forties. England, Scotland, or no, the "ain'ts and "hain'ts"

of Hardwick's generation were carried over into that of Mrs. Mathers-Briggs. In her son's head, the sounds of the hills commingled with its urban equivalent—the "Yo's" and "What what whats" punctuating urban Negro speech, which, though speeded up, carried the same possibility for expression as "hit's down yonder."

Every poet begins with the word. But every *epic* poet begins with the word as it shapes and reflects his or her world and thus *the* world. At home, or homes—when Mathers was nine years old, Mrs. Mathers-Briggs and her son moved to Roseville, another "white trash" dumping ground surrounded by Detroit's black underclass—there was a certain insistence on Mathers' mother's self, her "I." The drama queen spun fantasies about her physical and mental abuse while she wiped her hangover vomit off the Formica counter top in the small efficiency; meanwhile, her son developed his imagination.

Mrs. Mathers-Briggs' identification with Marshall was, from the first, complete, and, as they say, "inappropriate." This is not an uncommon phenomenon if one has given birth to a child while still a child. For women like Mrs. Mathers-Briggs, parenting doesn't end with providing food, shelter, the odd scrap of affection or worry, before sending your child into the world. Mother becomes synonymous with Wife, and the child is thought of as a Husband. Or, at least, the kind of husband she can identify with, since he is small and defenseless and feminized by the tyranny of poverty and Daddy-need, too. Just like Mommy.

But the relationship shifts. The child, the tiny husband, may grow up and speak out about the drama of his upbringing, his marriage, to this wife that was his by birth, not choice. And in language not too far, in tone at least, from Mrs. Mom's. "Put yourself in my position," Mathers raps on "Cleaning Out My Closet," one of the strongest tracks on *The Eminem Show*. "Just try to envision witnessin'/Your Mama poppin' prescription pills in the kitchen, bitchin' that/ Someone's always goin'/through her purse and shits missin'/ Going through public housing systems/Victim of Munchausen's syndrome, my whole life I was made to believe I was sick when I wasn't."

As autobiography, this is interesting. Mathers' "I" doesn't declare itself until the fifth verse. By that time, we've seen the pills, the kitchen, the public housing system; we've understood the symbolism of Munchausen's syndrome. And we've gleaned Mathers' sorrow and anger over feeling practically non-existent amidst his mother's (at times) overwhelming demands and addictions. These narrative steps and the kind of emotional leaps and connections they allow the listener to make are typical of Mathers' work, and accounts for the force and universality of his poetry.

Had Mathers merely relegated himself to the small, secular world he and his Mom shared, he would be yet another poet of domestic calamity talking about "viciousness in the kitchen!," as Sylvia Plath wrote once. To widen the scope of his work and give it a novelistic sweep that has generally been the province of folk music, not rap, Mathers had to marry something other than Mom, as it were. He had to connect the petty grievances to other more profound grievances—namely those of whites against blacks in Detroit, Michigan, where he still lives.

During World War II, nearly thirty years before Mathers' birth, Detroit was known as the "arsenal of democracy." Instruments of war such as guns and jeeps were produced there at a higher rate than anywhere else in the U.S., which meant that factory manpower was always in demand. Southern Blacks made their way north in search of better jobs; they assumed that by moving to cities like Detroit, Chicago, and New York, they would be escaping the lash of racism. And there was the hope that in the North blacks would be able to foster and keep close what had always been threatened in the South: the black family.

But by 1943, Detroit's 200,000 black residents had been crammed into sixty square blocks in the city's East End. There, they lived in deplorable filth. The black scourge threatened to spill over into the city's white, moneyed community. White politicians, hoping to keep them out, used dubious legal means to protect "their" community. They developed new city ordinances. They developed arbitrary county lines. They also built, along Eight Mile Road, where blacks lived in close proximity to whites, a wall six feet high and one foot thick. Civil liberties at a dead end.

To insist that the black underclass live in the urban equivalent of slave quarters implied a return to the old order: slaves over there, masters over here. Among blacks, this attitude generated rage, and a need for destruction. The race riots in the summer of 1943 were an outgrowth of a number of these long festering indignities. By the summer of 1943, "Liberty and justice for all" had become, for black Detroit, something of a joke. Liberty for whom? Justice from what? By the 1950's, twenty-three percent of the city's white citizens had moved to the suburbs. The industries that sprang up during World War II no longer needed as many workers because production had slowed since the end of World War II. Automobiles were being manufactured, but there was an excess of manpower

In 1967, rioting again broke out in the city. By then, urban planners had added "progress" to their list of affronts against blacks. Paradise Valley, a black community also known as "Black Bottom" had been razed prior to the riots to make way for Interstate 75, another road out of the city for those, white or black, who could manage it.

In the meantime, there was violence and dancing in the

streets. Bricks were thrown through shop windows, arrests were made, blood was shed, and young black men were stopped by cops who, if they didn't like their looks or what their looks projected—fear, resentment, disgust—re-arranged their young faces with billy clubs, and maybe a little spittle on the lips and eyelids

While Mrs. Mathers-Briggs was subjecting her husband by birth to her various psychological illnesses and heartbreaks, Mathers was reading the dictionary with the TV on, looking for words to describe his world, where blacks and whites had nowhere to go but their respective trailers, and nothing to imagine but their segregated poverty. How had things come to this? Did blacks and whites not have the same aspirations when the war presented all the able-bodied poor with new economic possibilities? Perhaps the dream was not the same after all. Perhaps, on the road north, white workers who had also come up from the south dreamt of no longer being part of the permanent underclass, and therefore not so closely identified with niggers. Perhaps, on the road north, black workers dreamed that city life would be the great equalizer, and that skin color would no longer matter.

As it turned out, upper-and middle-class whites—that is, white-collar workers—didn't much identify with blacks or poor whites. By the 1950s, it had become clear that white manual laborers could only hold on to the dream of whiteness by living among their own kind. In "If I Had," one of fifteen tracks on his 1999 album, *The Slim Shady LP*, Mathers writes from the perspective of the dude with the Confederate flag tied around his head, dreaming of restitution. "I'm tired of being white trash, broke and always poor," Marshall says. "Tired of taking pop bottles back to the party store/I'm tired of not having a phone/Tired of not having a home to have one in if I did have it on/Tired of not driving a BM/Tired of not working at GM."

Mathers' elders could not keep blackness away from their children, who had to attend the city's public schools, which were predominately black. There, Marshall found his voice—in black music. He also ran up against race hatred.

When he was twelve years old, a black classmate attacked Mathers a number of times—at recess, in the school bathroom. Once, the same bully knocked his skinny white victim down with a heavy snowball; Mathers sustained severe head injuries. Subsequently, Mathers' mother filed a claim against the school, saying that the attacks also caused her son to have debilitating headaches, intermittent loss of vision and hearing, nightmares, nausea, and a tendency toward anti-social behavior. The lawsuit was dismissed in 1983, when a Macon County judge in Michigan declared that public schools were immune from such lawsuits.

Mrs. Mathers-Briggs failed litigation was about her failure at language. Unlike her son, she never learned to control it. How could she not bend the law to her will? Her hysteria, telling tales about her victimhood, had worked on Marshall, making other kinds of knots in his head. Why should the courts be any different? (Her tendency to treat the wrongs that had been inflicted on her son and thus herself as an occasion for a public airing was not restricted to Mathers' defense. Indeed, after her son's second album came out, his mother sued him for defamation of character.)

Mrs. Mathers-Briggs had a penchant for exhibiting the knocks and bruises incurred by living in the most public ways imaginable. Just like an American. Mathers' inheritance was the Mrs. Mathers-Briggs show. He brought it with him when he left her to marry his audience. But he refined her hysteria, controlled it, gave it a linguistic form. By becoming an artist, he separated from Mother. He served her divorce papers by making records. Once he did so, Mrs. Mathers-Briggs could no longer imagine sitting in the trailer with her little husband, that beautiful white-haired wimp, coloring in his coloring books, dictionary open before him, reading about the roots of the English language while the TV blared. A Mom that is your Mrs. can never forgive you for believing you are someone different. That separateness belies her existence.

That the slings and arrows of Mathers' outrageous misfortune in and out of school, in and outside of Detroit's black world, did not deter him from falling increasingly in love with black music, is a testament to his interest in and commitment to exploring difference. Unlike many of the whites he grew up with, Mathers never claimed whiteness and its privileges as his birthright because he didn't feel white and privileged. Being emotionally beaten up at home, having his ass kicked at school, slinging hash in a number of fast food joints after he quit school in the 9th grade, all contributed to Mathers' sense that he was about as welcome in the world as any black man. And rap's dissonant sound was the soundtrack to all that. The music's form—with its barrage of words and double-entendres, shouting and silence, conversation and singing—was as familiar and natural to the burgeoning artist as the short story form was to Flannery O'Connor.

That Mathers should be open to a musical culture not his own is interesting. For some artists—white as well as black—there is the sense that delving into "otherness" allows them to articulate their own feelings of difference more readily. One thinks of the white, French-born photographer and art director, Jean-Paul Goude, and his 1978 masterwork, *Jungle Fever*. The book is a visual diary of Goude's fascination with and exploration of the world of colored women—black American,

Puerto Rican, Tunisian—and their erotic pull on Goude's imagination. *Jungle Fever* is as emotionally explicit as Mathers' lyrics. Like Goude, blackness made Mathers feel alive, present as an artist.

To say, as many critics have, that whites steal from blacks who originate important work in music or fashion is beside the point. Black American style has had a prevailing influence on the way Americans dress and create music for more than thirty years now, ever since Black Panther wives were covered in *Vogue* in the nineteen-seventies. What makes Mathers particularly annoying to his detractors is his brave acknowledgement of how whiteness sells blackness. In "White America," which appears on *The Eminem Show*: Mathers says:

> Look at these eyes, baby blue, baby just like yourself, if they were brown, Shady lose, Shady sits on the shelf, but Shady's cute, Shady knew, Shady's dimple's would help, make ladies swoon baby, {ooh baby}, look at my sales, let's do the math, if I was black, I would've sold half.

Of course, part of Mathers' genius lies in his ability to market his story to the white counterculture. He knew he wasn't the only wigger out there with a love of black music. From the beginning, he wrote for the white counterculture as much as he produced music that blacks could identify with. This bears some resemblance to Sly Stone's marketing technique in the early nineteen-seventies. Sly produced funk, but his lyrics were all about love, peace, and understanding. He made black dance music for white hippies.

Nowhere in his music does Mathers ever claim he wants to be black, like some sad, inner city Elvis. Critics that assume he does are missing the point, along with so much else. In the superficial writing that has grown up around his white hair and white T-shirt, the pathos at the heart of his lyrics is glided over if not missed altogether. His "rage," is that of the disillusioned romantic. Mathers can't quite believe the world is the world. Nor can he believe there's not enough love in it—especially for him. He writes with the hyperrealistic vividness of the romantic who can recall every slight, real or imagined. On "Kim" a song about his estranged wife, which appears on *The Marshall Mathers* LP, Mathers sends this letter from home:

How could you?
Just leave me and love him out the blue
Oh, what's a matter Kim?
Am I too loud for you?
Too bad bitch, your gonna finally hear me out this time
At first, I'm like all right
You wanna throw me out? That's fine!
But not for him to take my place, are you out you're mind?
This couch, this TV, this whole house is mine!
How could you let him sleep in our bed?
Look at Kim
Look at your husband now!

The operative word here is "look." Given Mathers' background, where all eyes were turned on Mom as she made scenes, could Mathers feel he was real? That he existed? Moms and bullies sucked all the air out of the room. In order to be heard, he did what born writers do: he began to write. And like most born performers, he longed for his work to be seen. As a teenager in Detroit, he began rapping on the under-ground music scene, where he made a name for himself. He released an album, but it didn't do much. He was given a sec-ond chance at fame when the music producer and rapper, Dr. Dre, got a hold of the disc, liked the lyrics, and commissioned Mathers to record something else. He was given the money and time to fine-tune his sense of difference through the hard work of making words carry meaning in a country where intel-lection is viewed with suspicion. Yet instead of looking at Mathers' words—the core of his art—which would generate analysis, discourse, a complicated response, his gang looks at his public persona, which is relatively simple. He's the rude American boy with a class chip on his shoulder. But what does that boy see, feel think? Why the anger over how humanity has fucked up the Garden of Eden, a place that is nothing if not a metaphor for love. Love of man for woman, black for white, all the things Mathers feels he has seen too little of.

Instead, he looks for love in the music. At present, he pro-duces the black rapper, 50 Cent. So doing, he mentors black-ness. A movie could be made of all this. Such a movie would begin with Mathers' birth as an artist. As one of the few icons this country has produced in the last decade, its not too far a stretch to imagine him as the love child of Marilyn Monroe and Bob Dylan. (That is, if her hysteria had not gotten the best of her and his self-regard the best of him.) Like Mathers, these icons came out of nowhere to change how we think about women, sex, lyrics, the voice. And in the process they told us something about ourselves. Sam Peckinpah, the mas-ter of blood and grit and male vanity, could direct this flick. Imagine Mathers in the film as a boy who adores his white trash mother. Mathers could sing a song—not one of his own. Perhaps a song from Lee Brier's brilliant stage play *Gospel at Colons*, one that is as autobiographical as anything Mathers has ever written: "Who is this man? What is his name? Where does he comes from? What is his race? Who is his father? Who is his father?"

In such a movie, Mathers would be presented as a new kind of star, a new kind of American. White on the outside, black on the inside, a boy in love with an ideal that he's still searching for, out there in the Garden.

WHITE
NOISE

EMINEM'S DIRTY SECRETS

by M.L. Elrick

from *salon.com*, July 25, 2000

he's a white boy who sounds black, a fatherless child who hates his mother, a trailer-trash wunderkind who spent some of his first millions on a king-size crib across from a mobile-home park.

Freud would have a field day with Marshall Bruce Mathers III. Rapper extraordinaire, record-setting, multi-platinum recording artist, gay-hater, murder-fantasizer, rebel and creep: How did this onetime "Mork & Mindy" devotee become the venom-spitting hero of hip-hop?

First came the runty Marshall Mathers, a quiet, artistic kid bounced from school to school by his overprotective, slightly unhinged mother. Then came "M&M," later Eminem, the silver-tongued outcast who forsook fitting in with his white suburban classmates to concentrate on breaking into Detroit's overwhelmingly black rap scene. Finally, and most furiously, came Slim Shady, the vile, rhyme-sayin', bitch-slayin' MC out to even every score run up against his other selves.

Yet none of these personas has canceled the other out. While Slim Shady rakes in the cash by rapping about rape, drugs and murder, Eminem tries to explain that it's all just an act—and 27-year-old Marshall Mathers struggles to hold together a world on the verge of being torn apart by the stress of success, run-ins with the law and, most recently, his wife's suicide attempt.

His 1999 album, "The Slim Shady LP," introduced the world to an implacable bleached-blond rapper who shot out his rhymes machine-gun style. It sold 3 million copies. His second album made him a sensation. "The Marshall Mathers LP" sold more than 5 million copies in its first month of release, becoming the fastest-selling hip-hop album of all time. MTV declared a weekend of "EmTV"; at the same time, some critics and gay groups began to take issue with the rank misogyny and homophobia permeating the album.

Eminem's defenders—and Eminem himself—say it's the Slim Shady character, not Mathers, who is the album's real culprit. But police arrested Mathers, not Slim Shady, June 4 in Warren, Mich. He'd found his wife, the former Kim Scott, in the parking lot of a nightclub, kissing an acquaintance. Eminem allegedly clocked the interloper with a 9mm pistol and threatened to kill him.

Eminem was arrested and faces an Aug. 31 preliminary hearing at which a Warren district court judge will decide whether there's enough evidence to send the case to trial. His alleged victim, John Guerra of nearby Mount Clemens, sued Eminem less than a week after the incident. As if he didn't have enough legal entanglements, Eminem has also agreed to stand trial in Pontiac, Mich., on charges he flashed his 9mm

outside a car audio shop during an argument with an associate of a rival rap group, Insane Clown Posse. The prosecutor
in the Warren case seeks at least a six-month sentence.

A few weeks after the throw-down in Warren, Kim Mathers
attempted suicide—just hours after Eminem finished the second of two performances in the Detroit area. Did she really
want to end the life her husband had already snuffed out on
both his albums? Did she want to leave the couple's 5-year-old
daughter motherless? Kim Mathers isn't saying. All she told
police who came to her rescue was, "There has got to be a better place than this." If nothing else, the incident was another
reminder that the emotional horrors recounted in explicit
detail on Eminem's albums may be more than mere shock art.

Just how Eminem feels about all of this is unclear, but a
comment he made to the Detroit Free Press during the filming of the video for his in-your-face anthem "The Way I Am"
might be apropos:

"Whenever something good happens, the bad always follows," he said. "That's the story of my life since the day I was
born."

life was a struggle for Marshall even *before* he was born. His
mother, Debbie Mathers-Briggs, says she married his father,
Marshall Mathers Jr., when she was 15; less than three years
later, she almost died delivering her first son at the end of a
73-hour labor.

"I went through a living hell," she said in a recent phone
conversation, recalling the bald, cigar-smoking St. Joseph,
Mo., doctor who charged $90 for prenatal visits, delivery and
circumcision. Marshall was a small, sickly baby.

Although Marshall was a well-behaved infant, Mathers-
Briggs said their life was never easy. The family moved to

North Dakota, where his father was supposed to take a job as assistant manager at a fancy hotel. What Mathers-Briggs contends was her husband's erratic behavior forced her to flee when her son was two. She says she left with Marshall in a rush, leaving their clothes and car behind when they lit out for her mother's home in Missouri. The Matherses divorced in 1975. Eminem's father, who later became a hotel manager in California, could not be reached for comment.

After several years in which he was doted on by his father's aunt while his mother held down several menial jobs, Marshall and his mother moved to Michigan. The pair lived in modest, working-class Detroit neighborhoods a notch or two above, but never far from, the ghetto. For many years he was the only white teen in a black neighborhood of otherwise white and middle-class St. Clair Shores. Friends and family said Marshall was a happy kid who had his mother wrapped around his finger. But he was also a bit of a loner—the kind of kid who got picked on.

As a 9-year-old student at Dort Elementary School, Marshall suffered the first in a series of beatings that ultimately left him in a coma, relatives say. His persecutor was DeAngelo Bailey, an African-American classmate who played center on the school basketball team. Bailey allegedly subjected Marshall to a four-month reign of terror: He attacked him at recess, cornered him in a restroom and floored him with a heavy snowball that gave him a severe head injury.

According to a lawsuit Mathers-Briggs filed against the school in 1982, Bailey beat her boy so badly that he suffered headaches, post-concussion syndrome, intermittent loss of vision and hearing, nightmares, nausea and a tendency toward anti-social behavior. (The lawsuit makes no mention of the coma, however.)

Marshall's head injury "made me even more protective of him," Mathers-Briggs says.

The lawsuit was dismissed in 1983; a Macomb County (Mich.) judge said the schools were immune from lawsuits. But Slim Shady settled the score 17 years later, beating Bailey into a bloody pulp on "Brain Damage," a track from his debut major-label album, "The Slim Shady LP."

The beefy, 5-foot-8 Bailey is now a laborer who lives in a squalid house near the neighborhood where the pair went to school. As Eminem's music booms out of a nearby car, he sits in a Roseville park and chuckles at the mention of his former whipping boy.

"He was small, plus he had a big mouth," recalls Bailey, who is married with four children.

Seeming friendly and soft-spoken, Bailey says he is amused by his secondhand celebrity. He says he has signed autographs for teeny-bopper fans and has had to disconnect his phone. His kids are big Eminem fans; they holler, he says, when Eminem mentions his name on "Brain Damage."

Bailey is sheepish but amused by the fruits of his former bullydom: "Damn, that must have scarred him for life," he says.

Marshall's life of childhood poverty in and around metro Detroit's hardscrabble neighborhoods continued. He bounced from school to school: By the time he enrolled in Warren's Lincoln High, he had attended as many as 20 schools, his mother estimates. Much of that time he lived in his great-grandmother's home on the south side of Warren, a gritty suburb just across the Detroit border.

Warren's residents are known for their red necks as well as their blue collars; the town's south side is particularly low-rent. Small houses are packed together along streets named for long-dead auto pioneers and lined with long-dead autos.

M.L. ELRICK

It's a short walk to the liquor store from most homes. Lonely hearts needn't go far to find the local adult bookstore or, a bit further along "8 Mile," a major boulevard dividing Warren from Detroit, prostitutes and topless bars with names like the Booby Trap and Trumpps.

Slim Shady is the kind of tough guy who callously advocates shooting a withered cashier and raping a 15-year-old. But friends and neighbors remember Marshall Mathers as a polite boy—one who comes back every so often to sign autographs and encourage neighborhood kids.

"He was an all right kid, no worse than a lot and a lot better than some," says Ramona Dorsey, who lives next door to Eminem's former house in St. Clair Shores.

"He was good to his brother," says Rose Slone, another former family friend who knew Marshall from when he visited his mother and brother in a rundown Warren trailer park. "He was always there for Nathan."

Former co-workers, too, said Marshall was hard-working and upbeat, playing music and rhyming to keep things lively. Until his arrests in June, Eminem had no adult criminal record.

As a 20-year-old, however, Marshall was arrested for an involvement with a drive-by shooting—with a paint ball. A friend was the triggerman, and the paint ball didn't even break, police said. The case was dismissed after the alleged victim didn't show up for court.

But his home life was seldom stable. Mike Mazur, Marshall's manager when he worked at a local restaurant, recalled that he crashed so often with friends—reportedly because of fights with his mother—that he had dozens of addresses in the more than three years they worked together.

But Mathers-Briggs bristles at any suggestion that she was less than an ideal mother. "Anything Marshall wanted he got," she now says from St. Joseph, where she runs a taxi service. "I sheltered him too much and I think there's a little resentment from that." Mathers-Briggs says she took care of her son's cleaning, car insurance and bank accounts until he was about 25.

But court records and interviews indicate that there was plenty of turmoil, too. A welfare mom who volunteered in a recent conversation that she once filed for bankruptcy, Mathers-Briggs has a history of settling disputes with lawsuits. While some neighbors remember her as a sweet and devoted mother, others called Mathers-Briggs irrational or, less charitably, "crazy" or "a bitch."

Marshall's former co-workers remember her calling him constantly at the restaurant, demanding to speak to her son even during peak times when he couldn't come to the phone. St. Clair Shores police said she often summoned them with unfounded complaints about neighbors.

Eminem does not recall his mother fondly. On "The Slim Shady LP" and in several interviews, he accused his mother of grabbing chunks of his paychecks, tossing him out and popping pills. She has steadfastly denied the allegations.

But the most damning accusation came from St. Clair Shores school officials, who in juvenile court proceedings in 1996 accused her of abusing her younger son, Nathan, now 14. Nathan was removed from her custody. Alleging that she "exhibits a very suspicious, almost paranoid personality," a social worker suggested that Mathers-Briggs had Munchausen syndrome by proxy, an affliction in which a parent injures a child to gain attention and sympathy for herself.

School officials also said she accused neighbors of beating Nathan, blowing up her mailbox and killing her dog in a satanic ritual. They added that she told them video cameras were monitoring her from trees outside her house and that enemies had sent her a tarantula in the mail.

Mathers-Briggs pleaded no contest to reduced charges that she was emotionally unstable and had failed her son by keeping him out of school and isolating him from other children; with that, she regained custody. By then, Nathan had been in foster homes for more than a year.

Attorney Betsy Mellos, who represented Mathers-Briggs through much of the court battle, says the school brought the charges because the mother had threatened to sue them. "She was a pretty good mother," contends Mellos, who now prosecutes child abuse and neglect cases for Macomb County, Mich. "If anything, she was overprotective."

The rest of the milieu around the future star wasn't much better. Marshall's male role models were his mother's boyfriends—one of whom left Mathers-Briggs after learning she was pregnant with Nathan—and his uncles. Todd Nelson, Mathers-Briggs' brother, served six years in a Missouri prison for manslaughter after a fatal fight with the brother of his wife. The couple moved to Michigan after his release, but are now divorced. Eminem is still in touch with Nelson.

But Marshall was closest to his uncle Ronnie, a sensitive soul who family members said was so repulsed by guns he was kicked out of the U.S. Army. Not much older than Marshall, Ronnie introduced his nephew to rap before dying from a gunshot wound about 10 years ago. The death was ruled a suicide.

By the time Eminem attended high school, his love of rap and black culture were the only things that distinguished him. "He hung around with a different kind of crowd than I did; I don't want to say rougher, but not really a good crowd," said classmate Eric Reiter, who remembered the otherwise unremarkable Marshall rapping confidently as part of a duo at a school talent show.

Another classmate, Aubrey Moylan, was less impressed. Calling Marshall "a dork," she says, "He came off as trying to be a poseur or a wannabe. He was into the whole rap scene even back then, and would try to imitate their style, speech and movements.

"He was the type of person that would have me rolling my eyes, thinking, 'Good grief, get a life.'"

Little did she know that's precisely what Mathers was doing.

Marshall dropped out of school in 1989. Mike Ruby, his partner from the talent show, recommended that he join him cooking and washing dishes at Gilbert's Lodge, a rustic, family-style St. Clair Shores restaurant. Neither rapper planned on making a career of the $5.50-an-hour gig.

A friend and fellow rap enthusiast from this time, Jay Fields, says that around 1990, Marshall and his partner in rhyme began recording scores of tracks in Ruby's basement. The future superstar was then calling himself M&M, later modified to Eminem. Using an insurance settlement, Ruby, who called himself Manix, set up a basement studio his crew dubbed Basement Productions, says Fields, who now works for a DJ service in Louisville, Ky.

"They were working on music back then, basically working on music everyday," says Fields, who at the time was known as Vitamin C. "[But they were] not getting anywhere because there was no promotion, just musical talent."

At first, Fields says, Eminem was just a smartass cracking inside jokes with Manix and his cronies. Before long, however, he said Eminem began teaching him what he called "the inside rhyme." "At that time, if you had two lines that rhymed, that was it," Fields says. "Marsh was putting it to the next level. He was trying to put as many words that rhymed into a line as he could fit."

But when Eminem finally decided to make his inside rhymes outside Manix's basement, he found few receptive audiences. Black folks, Eminem and associates have said, just weren't willing to listen to a skinny white dude rhyming—regardless of his talent.

So Eminem became a battle MC, trading insults with anyone who would take him on, honing his skills at largely black venues like the Hip Hop Shop, a now-defunct fashion and music boutique on Detroit's northwest side.

"He was getting in everybody's ass. It was kind of political at first, because he was an outsider," says House Shoes, a DJ at St. Andrew's Hall, a cornerstone of the Detroit music scene. "After he bit a few heads off people, it got to the point where people looked forward to him coming out there."

Eminem got his first break when a local producer, Marky Bass, heard him freestyling on a Detroit radio station. Within hours, Eminem was in Bass' studio rhyming. "He was phenomenal," Bass recalls. "I dropped everything I was doing and I put everything I had into this kid." Bass helped Eminem put out his first record, "Infinite." But no one cared. "Infinite" was filled with tracks about love, unity and trying to get on in spite of hard times.

While his career was stuck in neutral, Eminem's personal life was veering off in new directions. The most important relationship of his life seems to be with Kim Scott. His mother says she took in Scott, who had left her family home, around 1987, when she was 12 and Eminem was a few years older. After several years, Eminem and Scott started an on-and-off relationship, one that lasts to this day. They had a daughter, Hailie Jade, now five, and were married in 1999.

Mazur, Eminem's manager at the restaurant, says Eminem even gave up music to support his family. Although Eminem had been fired a few times for tardiness and other minor offenses—he was once canned shortly before Christmas—Mazur says he became a model employee. He recalls a six-month period shortly after Hailie's birth when Eminem worked 60 hours a week. "He didn't want his daughter to grow up like he did, living from day to day and moving from week to week," Mazur says.

But Eminem was also thinking about a new musical persona. Tapping into his reservoir of rage and resentment, Eminem created Slim Shady, a drug-dealing, bloodthirsty thug who spits furious rhymes about murder, rape, drugs and living by the law of the urban jungle.

Fields says he was shocked by his old friend's new persona. So was another Detroit rapper, Buddha Fulla Rhymes, he says. "Buddha asked [Eminem], 'Why do you rap about doing heroin and smokin' crack? This isn't you.' Marsh said, 'Look, I've been doing this for 10 years. I'm not making any money. I'm making pizzas.'"

As for Bass, he was thrilled when he heard of Eminem's recidivism. "We have the Marilyn Manson of rap, we have the kook of rap," he raved.

Bass wasn't the only one smitten by the reprehensible rapper. Gangsta rap impresario Dr. Dre heard Eminem rapping on an L.A. radio show around 1997. He brought Eminem to Interscope Records, the notorious home of some of the industry's hardest-core rap acts, and produced his first album.

By March 1997, Eminem was fired from Gilbert's for the last time. He was still living in his mother's mobile home with Scott and his daughter. But all that was about to change.

Eminem seems untroubled by issues of race. His best friends were (and are) black, and he swaggers easily in a black-dominated music genre. Racism is one of the few things he seems to take seriously. "That word [nigger] is not even in my vocabulary," he says in a recent issue of Rolling Stone. "I don't think you can put race alongside gender, or a man preferring a man."

He is less enlightened about the women he believes have done him wrong, however. (And notoriously even less so about gays.) He levels his most strident attacks at his women in general—and his mother and wife in particular. Whether it is because he is a spoiled brat scarred by being pushed out of the nest (as his mother and uncle contend) or the long-suffering son of an erratic shrew and manipulative wife, as he says, there's little love lost between Eminem and his mother these days.

Here's a sample of Eminem's feelings, from the track "Marshall Mathers" on the new "Marshall Mathers LP":

My fuckin' bitch mom suing for 10 million
She must want a dollar for every pill I been stealin'
Shit, where the fuck you think I picked up the habit
All I had to do was go in her room and lift up a mattress

Here's a lyric from "My Name Is" from "The Slim Shady LP":

Ninety-nine percent of my life I was lied to
I just found out my mom does more dope than I do
    (Damn!)
I told her I'd grow up to be a famous rapper
Make a record about doin' drugs and name it after her
    (Oh thank you!)

Hurt and angered by her son's allegations of abuse and drug addiction, Mathers-Briggs did indeed file a $10 million defamation suit against Eminem.

"People told me I'd be sorry someday," she says of the way she indulged her son, but she insists she isn't sorry. "Marshall is all for show, it's more put-on," Mathers-Briggs says of his attacks. "That's what everybody wants to hear."

Nelson, her brother, agrees. "His mother was real good to the boy," he said, adding that he never knew of any drug or alcohol abuse while Eminem was growing up.

But two of Mathers-Briggs' former boyfriends say otherwise.

"She is lying about the drugs and stuff," says Fred Samra Jr., Nathan's estranged father, whom Mathers-Briggs successfully sued for child support. "I won't say any more." Of Eminem, he said, "You would not believe the shit he has been through." Again, he declined to elaborate.

Don DeMarc, who says he dated and lived with Eminem's mother sporadically in the late '70s and early '80s, says Mathers-Briggs endured nagging pain, perhaps stemming from being hit by a car with a drunken driver. "She complained of headaches, backaches and toothaches," he says. "She always seems to be in pain. She's always looking for pain pills."

Mathers-Briggs denies allegations of drug abuse. Although she is a smoker, Eminem's mother said she raised her boy in a smoke-, drug- and alcohol-free environment. She says she is a member of Mothers Against Drunk Driving.

Eminem's travails with Scott, now his wife, are well known, too. On his new album, on the frenzied track "Kim," Eminem dispatches his wife in a bloody rage:

Don't you get it bitch, no one can hear you?
Now shut the fuck up and get what's comin to you
You were supposed to love me
[Choking sounds]
Now bleed! Bitch, bleed!
Bleed! Bitch, bleed! Bleed!

Former co-workers remember Eminem agonizing over his battles with Scott. "He would come in to work and worry and say, 'The bitch took my daughter and won't let me see her. I don't know what I'm going to do, I don't know what I'm going to do,'" said Mazur.

Fields said he remembers Scott picking a fight with Eminem minutes before he took the stage at a party celebrating the release of "The Slim Shady EP," the 10-track precursor to his breakthrough first major-label album. It was not a good time for a donnybrook, but Scott could not wait, Fields says.

Moments like that have not endeared Scott to Eminem's family. "She does not care about my son at all," says Mathers-Briggs. "She cares about the money." One of the less slanderous accusations Mathers-Briggs and Nelson hurl at Scott is that she has been arrested three times for drunken driving. (The Michigan Secretary of State's Office confirms two drunken driving arrests.)

Eminem's family also accuses his wife of feathering her own nest with proceeds from the rapper's phenomenal success, at their expense. Eminem and Scott own a spacious home in Sterling Heights; Kim's stepfather's name appears with Eminem's on the registration of a Ford Explorer, suggesting that it was a gift.

For their part, Eminem's mother says he reneged on an agreement to make payments on her Casco mobile home, which has since been repossessed. His uncle lives in the house his family has owned for 50 years and drives a 1987 Toyota pick-up truck pushing 200,000 miles. He insists that Eminem's family does not want money, only to free him from the grip of a gold digger and her manipulative family.

"A daughter is a daughter for life," Nelson says. "A son is a son till he takes a wife."

Kim Mathers did not respond to calls or letters seeking an interview.

After Eminem was arrested June 4 outside the nightclub where she says she gave an acquaintance a peck on the cheek, Scott denied cheating on her husband. "I don't think anybody in their right mind would cheat on a millionaire husband—especially with a nobody at a neighborhood bar," she says. In a letter to the Detroit Free Press, she wrote: "Just because my husband is an entertainer, that does not mean that our personal business is for everyone's entertainment purposes."

"I have always taken his word on things and stood by his side."

Referring to Eminem and Kim's relationship, Fields observed: "Pain, mystery and drama—that's what motivates an artist, as much as love and affection."

8 MILE

by William Bowers

from *pitchforkmedia.com*,
January 21, 2003

to borrow overwrought rhetoric from rap's meta-reluctant it-boy: Yo. If you had one shot—one opportunity—to state everything revolting about 8 *Mile* in one drunken rant, would you capture it, or just let it slip? Yo.

This will be my soggy goodbye kiss to "gangsta" material. I've got to cut it loose. The genre has produced some classics in its history (which could arguably be traced in its more interesting incarnations as moving from Ice-T to NWA to Tupac to B.I.G to Jay-Z to the contemporary crop, with various members of Geto Boys and Wu-Tang spread all around). I used to collect, laugh with, and love gangsta rap. Hell, I used to shoplift this stuff, religiously, if stealing can be considered a sacred ritual. But I've grown up. Gangsta has not. It gets

meaner, more covetous, and more puerile, as if its practitioners are serving sentences in a toxic never-neverland. I've even
heard a young MC (no relation to the soft, move-bustin hit-
maker Marvin Young) in NY admit that he hates the harness
of always being "hard." Gangsta's two artistic peaks were
Ready To Die and Cube's Bomb Squad-produced first solo
record. Now Biggie's dead and Cube is a lame comic actor
whose constant smiles cue savvy viewers into how his old
scowls were just mugging, entertaining.

Until gangsta says something new, I have nothing new to
say about it. I can't keep praising this stuff about torture and
murder as "brash storytelling." I am aware that *8 Mile*'s
Detroit can be a hell-on-earth; just this week it offered the
world news of street shootings, a dismemberment, a behead-
ing, and a underage forced prostitution ring. A friend there
told me of a factory worker spontaneously threatening to run
her over. I am not immune to the poetic justice of rap being
a conduit through which say, Detroit's denizens redistribute
their urban horror to the gated burbs; it's a thing of horrible
beauty, as beautiful—metaphorically—as cancer, in that cancer is often a manifestation of poisons in our habits or habitats
that drive our bodies to devour themselves. That disenfranchised Palestinian youth are reportedly turning to hip-hop to
voice their rage, striking indestructible gangsta poses, comes
as no surprise. But as Eric Boehlert asks in his essay on
Eminem, "Invisible Man," how long can critics give him a
free pass to say (and profit from) things that can be flat-out
anti-humanity? Could I praise some Aryan oi-core if it featured funny, tight anecdotes and really infectious grooves?
Isn't gangsta's violent reaction to its hells-on-earth the equivalent of pulling up to a socioeconomic drive-thru and getting
that hell super-sized? Where are the songs that pause and
reflect, like nineties artists were sure to include? These put-
upon souls often sound as if they're *enjoying* the blight.

In November 2002, the stage was set for a film to make a far-reaching argument for hip-hop's legitimacy: *The New York Times Magazine*, along with every other fad-rag, had done their buildup cover stories like "Why We Must All Teabag Eminem," piquing the curiosity of any Banana Republicans not yet in Marshall Mathers' tractor beam, and even the senior-discount demographic was guaranteed by Curtis Hanson's presence at the helm (director of the labyrinthine lite-noir *LA Confidential* and of *Wonder Boys'* antic blarney). Shoot, dogs, this film was flung at us by the producer of *Splash* and *Kindergarten Cop*—how could it fail? The fartsy-artsies were beginning to analyze Em as a supertext for the fear of an integrated planet. There was even a conspiracy theory that rap's white whale was secretly controlled by a cadre of cultural studies majors, his body floating suspended in testosterone above a circular table in their Whore Room.

Alas, *8 Mile* was Eminem's first major misstep as an artist. That sounds crazy, I know, on account of how much money it and its soundtrack will make and how it will help him win more Bruces, Eltons, and Vanillis, I mean Grammys, but now Slim is associated with a shoddy product, and he's become further entrenched in a synergistic feedback loop like his homiez (Ice Cube's spelling) Britney Spears and Mickey Mouse. No matter how "real" he is, now Eminem is a commercial for *8 Mile* is a commercial for Shady Records is a commercial for Eminem's albums is a commercial for MTV is a commercial for a "life style" is a commercial for Eminem is a commercial for…

Eventually the rule of *The Nightmare On Elm Street* will kick in: when Freddy was kept in the shadows, he was scarier and funnier, the rare bloodlusting molester just abstract enough to root for. But when sequels brought him into the daylight, and he was marketed as "scary!" and "funny!", he became a lame one-liner-spouting Alfism, another pop Proper

WILLIAM BOWERS

Noun, packageable in doll form to take up dumb space on our brain-shelves, where things like how our grandparents met were supposed to be stored. Eminem's undergone the same supersaturation; he even raps about it on this CD's "Rabbit Run" (the title of which must have John Updike golfing a little more righteously): "You're gonna hear my voice/ Until you're sick of it/ You ain't gonna have a choice."

But *8 Mile*, the film, was a trite turkey's turd that forgot to present anything virtuous about its protagonist, who mopes around with a sense of entitlement the size of a tricked-out Humvee. Eminem, though he's just as self-doubting, solipsistic, motor-mouthed, death-obsessed, mom-complicated, and preoccupied with leaving bodies in his wake as Hamlet, failed to erupt into a captivating dramatis persona. You won't believe you paid to enter this film's world. The plot and characterization were incoherent when they weren't generic. The guys of course prefer making war to making love, though the film includes a sex scene creepily shot in the you-are-there, watching-them-have-sex mode. The "touching, soft" scenes with the baby sister, Sympathy Ploy, beg the question of why so many people bother to act thuggy all the time. Seriously, why not just be like "hey, how you doing?" instead of "fuck all yall"? One of mainstream hip-hop's sad side effects is that whole culture of small-town kids too hardcore to drive their pajama-clad cousins out for ice cream in their Talons. Anyway, a lyricist's flow has to be majestic to transcend how trad-rap largely relies on a simple AA BB CC rhyme scheme, but *8 Mile* reduces rap battles to Def Insult Jams penned by a Dr. Seuss in a stained wifebeater: wow, he totally cussed out that other guy better than that guy totally cussed him out!

Strong points: the film's look is fittingly crappy, so bleak that you wonder what keeps the Detroit Chamber of Commerce from going through with that suicide pact. Also, Eminem maintains a great look of defeat during his factory job scenes. The plight of men in those warehouse walls is desperate, but it might not be as desperate as that of the people who made the Nike gear Eminem sports in angrily puckering pics all over the Internet.

The film's most uncomfortable ingredient is Eminem's ever-problematic whiteness. He is presented as magically, inexplicably distinct from all of the film's blacks—he's more complicated, more motivated, more talented, more attractive to others, etc. And of course, in the end, he must walk away from his (black) crew in order to find success. When I heard a bunch of diapersnake filmgoers and twinklestain critics compare 8 Mile's rush to that of Karate Kid and Rocky, I knew I was in the in the presence of a "racially coded" triumph. This isn't Eminem's fault, but when he (as Rabbit) rules that all-black room, it's not just an underdog victory-fantasy, but a victory-fantasy for whitey, winning another race's game/element. Like the first two Karate Kids and the Rockys, there's even a white-Jesus scene during which our hero takes a crucifying beating, from which he must resurrect himself. One is instantly reminded of the long tradition of special elastic whiteys that began circa Tarzan: whitey Kelly from Breakin, the white-blues Crossroads, the white ninjas (Dudikoff, Seagal, Norris), the white coaches/teachers/administrators who save the hood/tribe from itself (Wildcats, Hardball, Cool Runnings, The Air Up There, The Principal, The Substitute, Dangerous Minds), white suits who save the hood/tribe from itself (Ghosts of Mississippi, Mississippi Burning, Time To Kill, To Kill A Mockingbird) the pensive whiteys on the diverse frontlines of Nam (Sheen, Cruise, Fox), or the whiteys who soak up Native American traits or are burdened with preserving them (Dances With Wolves, Rambo, Windtalkers).

Hey! Have you ever heard a song called "Lose Yourself" by someone named Eminem? Whoo-doggie! An economist I know caught it on the radio and told me, "That tune's got legs." He's right! He said, "I kind of like hearing a song that inspires can-do self-mythology." Yup, for all its eye-of-the-tiger gusto, this song is basically the kind of numbing, socializing, everybody-gets-a-trophy propaganda that drips little doses of winner-haze into our rat cage. Think of a Smash Mouth anthem or some such "everything's alright" dross-ballad pumping into the cardiologist's lobby, while the spent husk of a receptionist on split-end-patrol fantasizes about her twenty-dollar Christmas-bonus gift certificate to Colonel O'McGillicuddy's Steak Hacienda Revenge.

Yet, "Lose Yourself" is inescapably bumping. Produced by Eminem himself, this track was designed to be appropriated by ESPN and blasted in bowling alleys on quarter-beer nights. Listen for the bulbous synth-hits and the echo on "you better never let it GO (Go) (go)!" The song was so readily and dramatically designed with the mass mind in mind that it sounds strange when you play it alone in your house; you'll end up in a stocking cap air-rapping, or staring out the window all sinister, villainous, and vulnerable, like you've got a master plan ain't nobody can replicate, but time's running out on it. *I kind of want to be beaten up to this song.*

The lyrics are of course just a summary of *8 Mile*'s subfascinating plot. But we can all relate to its paralyzing leisure-class problems: not having an arsenal of expensive clothes, not being famous, etc. The first lines about "there's vomit on his sweater already/ mom's spaghetti" = story of my life. "Lose Yourself" sets the tone for the album in that, while it sounds fantastic, its speaker thrives on gazing into the vacuum of his consumptive self-regard. All the songs (including the slow jams) on *8 Mile* exhibit wounded egos overcelebrating themselves.

Eminem's other two solo numbers cover the same Rabbit-saga as "Lose Yourself," though one allows him to spazz over a beat that recycles implosively like a snake with its end in its mouth, and the other is a threatening, symphonic lurcher that mentions rubbing poop on a woman's face. Again, these efforts are strong enough to make one wish that 8 *Mile*'s story didn't so pronouncedly fail to resonate.

The album's other selections ooze degradation. Women get hated, gays get bashed, and people either get threatened with murder, or murdered elaborately. I know that Pitchforkmedia.com often comes off like a Def Jux appreciation society, but that's because the Jukies realize how much more could be done vocally with the medium of hip-hop. Even this comp's frothing "angry" voices sound silly after spending a few months as a Jux addict.

And what could be more odious than an hour of bragging about who's the most hard, or soulless? All these guys are Old Testament Gods, striking down anyone who blasphemes their specious glory. Rakim praises Allah "to the fullest" on his most unhumble track, named after himself ("it's my crown, my world, my throne"). Xzibit yells "increase the hate," discusses his proficiency operating weaponry (flamethrowers, guns, grenades), offers some homo-cidal horrors and manages to reference Mexicans swallowing drug-filled balloons, how people defecate when they "get smoked," and how he knew spookiness "before the planes started crashing." Whew. Repeat plays of this song, for review purposes, have me and my friends about to get fetal like a shrimp cocktail and shiver until Armageddon tomorrow afternoon.

Eminem's petulant team-up with Obie Trice and 50 Cent is a putdown of humpy R&B that features such fetching proclamations as "we want to love alcohol, guns, and money, but not no bitches." Then Mr. Cent, whose magnetic flow could be best described as a really fast slur, expounds on authentically funny disses of Lauryn Hill, Lil Kim, R Kelly, D'angelo, and Ashanti. Before busting into pig latin on "Rap Game" with D12, Eminem rhymes "dick," "bitch," and

WILLIAM BOWERS

"shit"! Young Zee raps about dealing coke and drowning children! He raps about having sixteen cellphones and four pagers! He out"royals" the Taliban, he says! Please tell me his song is a joke or a conscious overstatement that I'm too reactionary to get! 50 Cent's two solo showcases have ended up being ironic, since they're about cars full of guns and how he won't go to jail ("not even to visit a nigga"). But two weeks ago he was arrested for having weapons in his car.

Jay-Z and Freeway's duet is literally a commercial for their upcoming albums. Nas' song just calls Jay-Z "you faggot, you bitch, you coward, you clown." Macy Gray's "Time Of My Life" (not a cover of the love theme from *Dirty Dancing*), while still boasting bizarrely self-centered lyrics, is so innocuous that it's refreshing. She of course sounds like a stoned mix of Dionne Warwick and AC/DC's Brian Johnson, and the song is so last-night-of-summer-camp that one can't help but picture her with a whistle around her neck handing out Cheez-Its and Kool Aid. The award for Funniest Moment goes to whoever raps last (and calls himself "retarded") on D12's contribution, namedropping BelBivDevoe, Garth Brooks, and Lorena Bobbitt with gymnastic hilarity. Gang Starr's big beat and bombastic cartoon-pimp horn-blasts barely edge out Rakim's pulsing off-time bone-stomp for Most Interesting Backing.

In fact, the wiry keyboards and drum-plods of the whole disc comprise a masterpiece of ominous miminalism, but the negativity contaminates the fun to be had bopping along to this stuff. How can you get loose in this terror-rific era while Eminem says he wants to blow up a building, and many of the others discuss shooting up crowded places? Get some therapy, dogs! Must be tiring to act like a heavy all the time. I know that chronicling street life is priority with these artists, but alls I'm saying is that limiting hip-hop to this tough-pose crime-costume junk is like only training horses to jump into rendering vats. These death threats make my tread-lightly indie-rock ass pine for Stephen Malkmus' "disses" of Smashing Pumpkins and Stone Temple Pilots. This album's turf is spotted with failures of its inhabitants' imaginations. To be the "indie rock" of the 00s, as many feel that hip-hop is, the gangsta branch is going to have to do something more revolutionary than play into the hands of the image-and-acquisition culture marketed to the mainstream, or at least stop enforcing the stereotypes of paranoia-breeding newscasts.

If Rabbit's I-want-it-therefore-I-deserve-it logic appeals to you, why not follow up your purchase of this indelicate opus by nabbing *More Music From 8 Mile*, which assembles songs from the film's mid-nineties milieu, rather than these "Inspired By"-type new songs. Inspired by! Hell, why not buy the "clean" version of this album just to hear if it beeps like a convulsive answering machine. I have to go; I'm being killed by Obie Trice.

WILLIAM BOWERS

NOISE

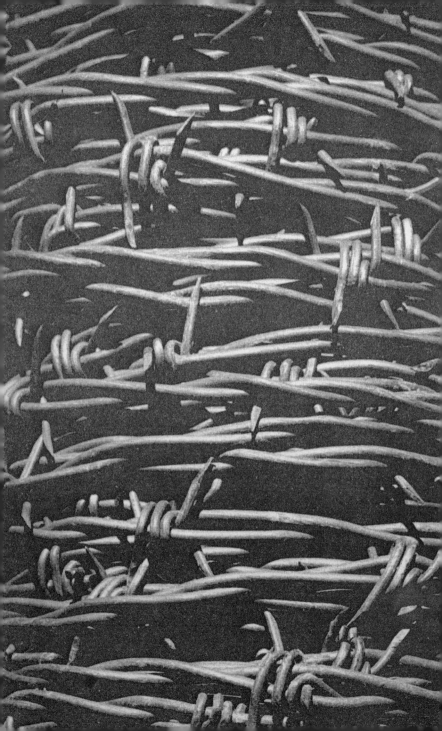

MORAL ABDICATION
or JUST FATHER-SON BONDING WITH A CREEPY EDGE

by Mark Cochrane

from *The Vancouver Sun*,
February 22, 2003

in the car my 12-year-old son and I listen to Eminem, and we know every word, every snarled and spit syllable. As fans of potty-mouthed, horror-show rapper Marshall Mathers III—aka Eminem, aka Slim Shady—my son and I could probably perform the entire CD from start to finish in a karaoke bar. Not since the days of Garbage Delight and Alligator Pie have we spontaneously committed verses to memory with such pleasure.

Sometimes while driving, however, I watch my son mouth profanities of a kind that would have been unimaginable when I was his age. Even more surreal to me, is the fact that I am tolerating, sharing and nurturing my child's enthusiasm for a renowned hate-monger. It's father-son bonding with a creepy edge. Or maybe it's just moral abdication.

At least I know I am not alone on the laissez-faire side of parenting. One evening last summer, when Without Me was on the airwaves, we pulled into the driveway with the windows rolled down and the bass turned up. When I shut off the engine, the bevy of boys and girls shooting hoops next door finished the song for us—verbatim, a cappella, and in the unexpurgated form, not the friendly "airplay" version. Since when did "cum on your lips & some on your tits" become playground singalong in Kits?

The combination of childishly catchy melodies with woman-hating lyrics (or bloody, imaginary dramas) is part of Mathers' allure. Yet this same track continues with a passage that I like to discuss with my Kwantlen college English students; among other things, it offers examples of how verbs and participles can create metaphors: I'm interesting, the best thing since wrestling/Infesting in your kids' ears and I'm nesting . . .

Mind-poisoning, kid-perverting earwigs. Children love this stuff, and my students always lift their foreheads from the desks whenever I mention Eminem by name.

Much has changed since the early '90s, when everybody I knew was a kneejerk-PC graduate student and my son was a newborn. But still the driveway episode left me with, say, conflicted goosebumps. Whatever its content, these kids were memorizing poetry—there is no better term to describe what Mathers produces—and no teacher or drama coach was force-feeding them. They were revelling in sound, metrical precision, wordplay and characterization: The pure wicked vivacity of Eminem's lyrical theatre. While playing horse with a basketball, they were paying homage to the living master of internal rhyme.

"Shut the hell up/I'm trying to develop these pictures of the devil/to sell 'em."

Whatever condemnation I might formerly have heaped upon Mathers for his views and lyrics about women and gays, no living poet confined to the page can touch what this bleach-blond brat has accomplished. Not even Canadian-born Classics professor Anne Carson, my other favourite poet, recently identified by critic Harold Bloom as one of a handful of "living geniuses," can approach the impact that Mathers continues to have on our literary culture, both highbrow and low. His virulent persona has taken the English-speaking world by the throat, even as he threatens to slash it.

And therein lies the dilemma. I am glad that my kids and my students gravitate to a wordsmith who takes his language-play so seriously. But his work and language is fundamentally concerned with hate speech and its connection to the self-conscious art of satire.

Tomorrow night he may lose the Grammy for Album of the Year to the long-snubbed Springsteen whose latest CD is a sac-charine snoozefest, but everybody knows that The Eminem Show is the most culturally significant album of 2002. And now Mathers also boasts an Oscar nomination, for the song Lose Yourself from his acclaimed, quasi-autobiographical film 8 Mile.

If he wins any of these awards, there will be outrage, because courting controversy is both Mathers' method and his subject matter. Everything we can possibly say about Eminem, his songs have anticipated. "I am whatever you say I am." All along the rapper has scripted both the reception of his work and the media analysis of that reception.

Mathers folds everything that transpires around him back into his writing, and this complex refraction—even the word "Eminem" is self-mirroring—is one of the reasons that the name of "genius" has not been misapplied by the legion of kids, and critical admirers, marching in back of him.

Eminem's oeuvre is rife with ironies and wit. The line

MARK COCHRANE

"Feminist women love Eminem," from the hit The Real Slim Shady, is not just infuriating and provocative falsehood—the sentence is also a marvel of assonance and consonance, recycled vowel and consonant sounds.

Yet, while many observers have caught a whiff of literary genius off Eminem's body of work, could Harold Bloom ever be convinced? Only, perhaps, if Bloom means what he says when he identifies vitality, audacity, originality and self-reliance as the hallmarks of genius.

Once more Anne Carson, who passes Bloom's test, offers useful comparison here, because at her worst she's as bad as Mathers. In Bloom's universe, however, a poet's candidacy for "genius" depends heavily on the quality of her allusions—the references he or she makes to cultural "authorities," and the tradition the poet aspires to. That's why Carson gets away with all kinds of dour vulgarity and downright sloppiness in her writing. Even as she beats to death the story of her broken marriage, she peppers her work with references to the Greeks—and to a myriad other great thinkers besides. She puts her learning to great subversive service.

Eminem's frame of reference, on the other hand, is confined to his own trashy and violent life—to sex, drugs, media . . . and his broken marriage. Like Carson, he makes brilliant use of the materials he's mastered, but self-centred pop cultural allusions, no matter how sophisticated in their puns and cross-referencing, don't buy you a shot at immortality, from the likes of Bloom.

Still, many writers in North America and the U.K. have credited Mathers with a resurgence of interest in the spoken and written word. Two years ago an article appearing in The Guardian compared Mathers with a number of canonical poets, most notably Browning and Eliot, great practitioners of the dramatic monologue.

A more recent article in *The New York Observer* suggests that "the Eminem flavour" can be discerned in novels by young Americans whose other influences include Dave Eggers and David Foster Wallace. Zadie Smith of *White Teeth* fame is an avowed fan. And Vancouver writer Lee Henderson, another Eminem-ophile, once pointed out to me that Mathers, on the track "Business," takes up the age-old poet's challenge of finding a word to rhyme with "orange." The result is a flurry of weirdly beautiful lines containing two such words: " . . . set to blow college dorm room doors off the hinges/oranges, peach, pears, plums, syringes."

Another article, on CNN.com, compares Marshall Mathers to Mark Twain, and suggests that Eminem's obscene ideas and vocabulary are analogous with the politically incorrect vernacular of *Huckleberry Finn*.

Are Mathers' alter egos—Eminem and the more diabolical Slim Shady—best understood, then, as fictional characters, unreliable first-person narrators, satirical personae? (*Spin* magazine once called this argument a "morally weak dodge" but nevertheless "totally legitimate.") Is Eminem Mathers' own Huck Finn, forever coming of age in the toxic street slang of his own time, lashing out at the world with that nasally, nerdish, pubescent twang?

Or is it, as opponents argue, that Eminem creates reprehensible characters in order to pass off his own reprehensible views? Satirical writing can still get a writer in trouble, and most readers recognize that "satire" can be a ruse for strafing your victims while avoiding litigation or moral accountability.

The best defence for Mathers I can muster is that he is a complete psychological mess, out loud, all the time. In the 1999 single *My Name Is*, Mathers' persona worries that his mother won't be able to breastfeed him because she has no breasts. Paging Dr. Freud.

But unlike some other rappers, Eminem tempers his boasts with a wounded vulnerability. Women cheat on him. His parents—disappearing gay father, pill-popping paranoiac mother—embarrass him. He feels insecure and, at times, just wants to give up. In 8 Mile, the film's hero Rabbit wins the rap "battle" by belting out a litany of personal humiliations and badges of shame. This climax, it seems to me, marks a triumph of the confessional mode: everything his opponent might say about him, Rabbit says first. Eminem's best cuts explore fear, loss of confidence and writer's block.

Like the great confessional poets (think Sylvia Plath), Mathers delivers a barrage of personality that transcends egotism to become a study in character and Oedipal psychosis. Like Plath, he achieves his effects through a discordant combination of singsong rhythms and harrowing imagery.

For Marshall—the bullied, reticent little dopehead—life is endless Junior High, a red haze of sexual jealousy and identity-panic. He captures the cacophonous inner life of boys with great lucidity. "I could be one of your kids," he threatens, and he is right. Still, critics, and parents, wonder why Mathers cannot flex his poetic muscles without also spewing hate. Why doesn't he keep the phat beats, the hooks, the cleverness, but jettison the verbal violence? Is it really true that hate is sexy, that hate sells? Aren't re-mixed, cleaned-up versions of his songs just as good, and far less scary?

Perhaps it's a simple fact of language, and performance: Rage rocks.

Ultimately, I think Eminem's work should not be measured against Bloom's genius template, but according the less bourgeois standards of "transgressive literature." In crossing social boundaries and rupturing liberal niceties, in his relentless quest to piss people off, Mathers belongs to a lineage whose work has always occupied the uneasy border between subversion and hatred, and whose imaginative freedom has always needed protection.

Eminem's work seems to function partly as an antidote to itself. Mathers demystifies hate speech through exaggeration, through the blatant silliness of his troublemaking. Indeed, what many kids seem to intuit, what my own son understands without being told, is that Eminem's attitudes are the ones right-thinking people are supposed to reject.

Even under the seductive force of Mathers' misdirected anger, kids can still get the joke. And they get it because of, not despite, the work's most disturbing elements.

Parents—if they are willing to listen to this music and examine it critically with their children—might consider Eminem immersion as a form of inoculation. As the kids in the driveway taught me, Mathers' ideas are virulent antigens that children will ingest whether they are shielded or not. Like us, they need to develop immunities in order to reject hatred in their world, even as they get a twisted kick from it in their music. It may not be quite the same twisted kick they got out of Garbage Delight or Alligator Pie, but ultimately, it might be more instructional.

MARK COCHRANE

THE BOY ON THE BUS

by Craig Taylor

from *Open Letters* 7/18/00

hello, Scott, you wily old man, with your highlighted hair and your little digital files. I finally received those audio clips, after about an hour of pacing around the attic watching my computer slowly download, waiting for the whole thing to crash. But yes, they all made it through, even the Eminem tracks, which is what I was most worried about. The only time I'm ever going to hear his album is on my computer. There's no way I can actually walk into an HMV and buy it without feeling extremely dirty. But what would you know? You're the one who wanted to send me that song where he's killing his ex-wife. I can't get past that. I'll listen, but I won't listen to track sixteen.

I feel like I've crossed some sort of Eminem threshold, though. When the first album was breaking out I had no idea who he was except for the posters on the walls of construction sites downtown. I heard the "Hi My Name Is" single at Cora's Pizza over on Spadina once while I was ordering, but that was it. Now I'm talking about him all the time—to Sean and Bill, and even to J., who admitted she didn't know too much about the guy and was more worried about the violence in Cypress Hill albums. I'm not holding it against her, but those guys were mild potheads with a couple bad samples, cartoony like Hammer. Any violence there was incidental. There's something different about Em.

Did you read that little blurb about him by Ben Greenman in the *New Yorker*? He said that Eminem's raps retain "a certain charm in part because of his indisputable poetic abilities and in part because his horrific imaginations seems so patently fictional." Which is fine to say if you're Ben Greenman, but I don't think all of Eminem's fan base agrees that it's fiction. Not to say that I'm scared of *everyone* who listens to the disc. Greenman will probably be fine. I'm more worried about the white kid who doesn't give a fuck, who isn't aware of Slim Shady's poetic meter or his place in a canon that goes back, way back, past Kool Moe Dee even. I'm not pulling a Tipper Gore and getting scared of an entire genre, but I am feeling a little wary.

The other day there was a kid on the bus that I take to work. When I got on, he was squatting down low inside his Ecko pants—the kind with the white reflective strips down the side. His headphones were like yours: those sleek, well-designed flashes of purple plastic, bent around the back of his head. To go over the top like headphones used to would mean he'd have to take off the Yankees hat. Not a black cap like the ones the clean-living pros wear, but light blue, identical to the real Slim Shady's. He was on the bus with a friend he liked well enough to let her stand near his squat. ("Shut up, bitch" was the first thing I heard him say to her, and at that point it was so outrageously misplaced that I laughed to myself). One of his hands was holding onto the chrome bus pole while the other was busy pulling and pushing on the crotch of his pants in that loose-limbed, bored style that someone's always using in the background of hip-hop videos.

The bus was packed. The racial breakdown was all over the map. Lots of dark skin, dark eyes. The Ecko kid and I were about the whitest: I'm pastier than usual now from working indoors all the time, and I was wearing an unfortunate blue dress shirt, untucked, and wet hair. We were all on our way to Don Mills, over the viaduct and out beyond the Jack Astor's restaurant.

All of a sudden, as we're passing over the Don Valley bridge, the crouching kid said, loudly, "People always trying to fuck me around," ostensibly to the girl beside him. But he was staring at me while he said it, and then at the man next to me, and then the man next to him. "Motherfuckers always trying to fuck me around." Someone turned the page of a paper, but no one else made a move. He lifted his face toward the two older black men who were sitting in the back seat. They both had high cheekbones and short buzz cuts, and were dressed in golf shirts, and were staring at their hands. "A nigga like me can't get any respect," he called out. "Ain't nobody giving it up." There was an absolute silence in the bus. I could hear the hydraulics of the wheels, and then the light "ting" of someone pulling the Next Stop cord, but nothing else. The two black men kept staring at their fingernails.

I have been trained, since becoming a Torontonian, to do what everyone else does in a situation like this: keep reading the free newspaper in my hands. I tried to catch a reaction from my fellow riders, especially from the other black man beside me, who was engrossed in his Sheridan College textbook. Nothing.

"What are you talking about?" said the girl standing beside Eminem. She was dressed in a light blue pull-over that matched the colour of his cap. And here's where it got truly scary for me. He acknowledged her in a way, nodding his head as if to say, "Shut the fuck up," and then put his two fingers together to form a gun, which he pointed at each of the passengers in the back. First at me, then at the Sheridan College man, until he had gone down the entire row. He started singing and moving to his song. It was a strange, menacing squat dance. "You don't. Want to fuck. With Shady. Cause Shady. Will fuckin' kill you. And you. And you."

I didn't know whether he was singing along to his walkman or if it was just a fitting lyric for the situation. I was probably the only one on the bus who recognized that it was Eminem— maybe not, who can say?—but it didn't matter. The words were his, and whatever fictional context they might have had on the album had been dropped. "I'll fucking kill you," he continued. "You don't. Want to fuck with Shady. Cause Shady. Will fucking kill you. And you, nigga." The man with the Sheridan textbook closed it and rang the Next Stop bell.

I read in Spin where Eminem described his triple-threat persona. Eminem is the rapper, Marshall Mathers is the man himself, and Slim Shady is the attitude that he assumes. It's an attitude that could just as easily be grafted on to boys in identical blue Yankees caps.

The boy and his girl spotted a McDonald's on Pape Avenue, and that was that. He pulled out of his squat, hitched his pants up, and said to her, "Ring the fucking ringer." She did. And when the bus stopped at the intersection and the doors swung open, the two of them stepped off.

Your brother,
in Toronto,
in the attic,

Craig

HE CAN'T KEEP SAYING THE SAME SHIT

by Alexis Petridis and Giles Foden

from *The Guardian*, May 24, 2002

today, it is *de rigueur* for major artists releasing a new album to receive a publicity blitz that stretches far beyond the usual interviews and reviews. Most content themselves with a tabloid splash based on their love life or a self-produced TV documentary highlighting their genius, munificence and, of course, their regular-guy humility. Such trifles, however, do not seem to fit Eminem. No new release from the rapper who can justifiably claim to be the world's most notorious recording artist would be complete without controversy.

This time, however, the storm is rather different. No one has attempted to sue him for defamation. No pressure group has accused him of penning "the most blatantly offensive homophobic lyrics ever" or compared him to Hitler, as Peter

NOISE

Tatchell did last year. As Marshall Mathers III readies his third album, The Eminem Show, the controversy stems from a more mundane source: internet piracy. The Eminem Show has been readily available for illegal download on the net for weeks. Last weekend, it was reported that bootleg CDs of the album were available on the streets of New York for a bargain $5. So widespread and serious is the result that his label has been forced to bring the release date forward by a month. Eminem himself has weighed in with the sort of sparkling and considered argument against internet piracy that Liam Gallagher would applaud for its eloquence. "I think that shit is fucking bullshit," he remarked. "Whoever put my shit on the internet, I want to meet that motherfucker and beat the shit out of him, because I picture this scrawny little dickhead going, 'I got Eminem's new CD! I'm going to put it on the internet!' I think that anybody who tries to make excuses for that shit is a fucking bitch." The man who wrote songs called Just Don't Give a Fuck and Still Don't Give a Fuck has apparently found a subject he gives a fuck about.

A cynic might suggest that the internet piracy palaver is a convenient way of detracting attention from the album's content. The Eminem Show certainly finds the rapper at an intriguing and crucial juncture in his career. The cliche of the "difficult third album" is rooted in reality. As the career of Oasis proves, fast-burning rock phenomena traditionally have two great albums in them: their debut, fuelled by success-hungry self-belief, and its follow-up, a kind of musical lap of honour powered by a beguiling, we-knew-we-were-right arrogance. By their third album, they find themselves rich, successful and contented—and lost for anything to say.

It's a problem that Eminem should feel more acutely than anyone else. No album in history articulated the frustration of life among America's trailer park underclass more luridly than his debut, 1999's Slim Shady LP. In the process Eminem redrew hip-hop's racial boundaries, proving the genre that had spoken for America's disenfranchised black population could be adapted to speak for its disenfranchised whites. Meanwhile, only Nirvana's swansong In Utero can match 2000's Marshall Mathers LP as a livid, self-baiting document of instant and unwanted celebrity. As the rapper Proof, of Eminem's Detroit crew D12, pointed out in a recent interview: "If he's still talking the same shit about how he's broke or wants to kill everybody, what would be the maturity in it? He's happy now. The motherfucker got some money. He can't keep saying the same shit."

Quite. Where does Eminem go now that he's established that his upbringing was turbulent and fame isn't all it's cracked up to be? Certainly his releases since The Marshall Mathers LP have suggested lyrical inspiration was running dry. Last year's album Devil's Night, recorded with D12, was dire, a collection of unfunny jokes about sex with the disabled and eating babies—all Eminem's censor-baiting nastiness with none of the vindicatory existential angst. The Eminem Show's first single, Without Me, casts desperately around for something to attack before settling on oafish nu-metallers Limp Bizkit and, unbelievably, Moby, who Eminem complains is too old and bald. You feel that if his targets were any softer, he'd be reduced to dissing Anthea Turner and the Andrex puppy.

Mathers, then, must be perversely grateful for the continuing attentions of his appalling family. Perhaps the solitary interesting point raised in his recent handful of reveal-nothing interviews came when the rapper remarked, "It's like I need drama in my life to inspire me a lot, instead of just trying to reach for something." Luckily, his mother has been on hand to provide plenty of that. Having made only $1,600 from her $12m defamation suits against The Slim Shady LP, Debbie Mathers further enraged her son by releasing a rap CD, Dear

Marshall, "to set the record straight". Her actions inspire The Eminem Show's Cleaning Out My Closet, a startling howl of rage set to dragging beats and arpeggiated guitar riffs familiar to fans of 1980s stadium rock. "Hailie's getting big now, can't you see that she's beautiful?" he barks, referring to his own daughter, his voice raw with emotion, "but you'll never see her, she won't even be at your funeral—how dare you try and take what you didn't help me get? You selfish fucking bitch, I hope you burn in hell for this shit."

Cleaning Out My Closet is over the top and uncomfortable listening, but it's difficult to remain unmoved by the sheer force of the track's anger. It is not hyperbole to suggest that no one in the pop arena has ever recorded anything quite as unsettling as this. Indeed, The Eminem Show is at its gripping best when its anger finds some aim. The lumbering opener, White America, comes laden with chugging rock guitars. It essentially reiterates the self-mythologising point of the 2000 single The Real Slim Shady: that Eminem speaks for a legion of disaffected white teens whom polite society would rather ignore—yet does so with eloquence and injured rage. "There's so much anger aimed in no particular direction, it just sprays and sprays," he raps. "Let's do the math: if I was black I wouldn't have sold half—my skin is starting to work to my benefit now." The album's remarkable stand-out track, My Dad's Gone Crazy, meanwhile, features backing vocals from his daughter—who makes chainsaw noises and does a disturbing impersonation of her father's voice—and returns to the subject of Debbie Mathers with a sharp wit: "As my mother always told me, nuuuuuh nuuuuh nuuuuuh."

When The Eminem Show simply tries to shock for the sake of it, however, the album flounders. Eminem may proudly boast of being the "bogeymonster of rap" but in the two years since he last released a solo album, the stakes have been raised. America has found some very real bogeymen, whose actions have proved far more shocking than anything even the most foul-mouthed hip-hop artist can offer.

On dreary tracks such as Solider and Superman, which mix meaningless references to September 11 with casual misogyny, there's a sense that Eminem is trying too hard to horrify. Drips even attempts to squeeze humour from Aids, revealing that as a satirist, Eminem is more Stan Boardman than Chris Morris. Curiously, the one taboo the album avoids is homophobia; replacing it are glowing accounts of his friendship with his Grammy duet partner Elton John. If there can be such a thing as platitudinous outrage, it is the currency of The Eminem Show's handful of low points. In addition, they undercut Eminem's attempts to take the moral high ground and present himself as a divorced parent who doesn't want to follow in the footsteps of own absent father, who "just wants to give Hailie the life I never had". It's difficult to take advice on family values from someone who elsewhere threatens to "put anthrax on your Tampax and slap you till you can't stand". And it's even harder to take Hailie's Song, a mawkish tribute to his daughter: "People make jokes, they don't see my real side," he croons mournfully—a bit rich coming from the man behind Drips.

The album's production, mostly handled by Eminem, is smartly done, and his often overlooked skills as a rapper are unquestionable. It is no difficult third album, yet like all of his albums to date, The Eminem Show is of decidedly variable quality. Bizarrely, it recalls nothing so much as the notorious Derek and Clive albums recorded by Peter Cook and Dudley Moore in the late 1970s. When it fails, it just sounds like someone swearing for no reason at all—it's not offensive, just boring. When it works, it derives something funny, disturbing and foul-mouthed from frustration and anger: it is hard to think of anyone producing rock or pop music more viscerally thrilling.

ALEXIS PETRIDIS and GILES FODEN

Eminem, according to online search engine Lycos, was at number two on the "web's most wanted" list for 2001. Number one was Osama bin Laden. From September 11 onward, the al-Qaida leader has entwined himself into the fabric of popular culture. Before that fateful day, Bin Laden received as few searches as the nation of Burkina Faso. He has since equalled his year 2000 search total every 7.5 hours.

But what a feast for the collective online mind if Eminem and Bin Laden were together? Obliging as ever, here's Eminem dressed up as public enemy number one in the video for his new single, Without Me. It's hilarious. But even for the "don of disgust", with his magisterial command of pop-cultural and other references, is this a step too far?

In the form of a cartoon strip, the video first presents Eminem as Batman's Robin, or "Rap Boy". Called from his bed, he has to save American youth from his own music. He drives across town with his sceptical associate, Dr Dre. The video also features D12 as Eminem's posse, and his new protege, Obie Trice. The variety of satirical targets ranges from the singer Moby—beaten up by a pink bunny—to that old favourite, Eminem's former wife Debbie.

Rap Boy successfully stops a young teenage boy, played by Eminem's half-brother Nathan, from listening to the new album, The Eminem Show, of which Without Me is the first single.

So far as the single itself goes, to some degree we're back with hero worship—back with Stan, Eminem's parodic hit about a doomed fan. The title of the new song is itself parodic. A stock phrase of the romantic ballad ("without you") is turned on its head and reapplied to popular craving for the singer himself.

It is, however, no longer just hero worship of the star that's involved (as in Stan), but the way Eminem "heroically" fills a gap in the American national psyche. "Now this looks like a job for me," says Rap Boy, girding his loins. "So everybody, just follow me/ Cause we need a little controversy/ Cause it feels so empty, without me." Eminem goes on to imply, in a clever piece of negative theology, that the media and his critics substantively depend on him.

The video also shows US vice-president Dick Cheney being electrocuted (last year his wife attacked Eminem's lyrics), and satirises an ageing, infirm Elvis Presley. It is suggested that the King owed just as big a debt to black music as Eminem does.

The Eminem satirical method becomes clear. It's a kind of triangulation—the political manoeuvre devised by Clinton's adviser Dick Morris, and later adopted by Blair—whereby one pulls opposition into one's own arena and thereby rises above it. Eminem himself becomes the instrument of Parental Advisory content, wagging his finger admonishingly.

In the Bin Laden sketch, donning a shaggy beard and camouflage fatigues, Eminem gets down to bhangra-like rhythms. The posse at first pursue and then join him, dancing in an ill-lit cave. Burlesquing one of the videos al-Qaida released last year, it is apparently shown on "ENN".

Is Eminem explicity associating his critique of America with that of Bin Laden, another "visionary, vision of scary"? Not necessarily. Just because Eminem dresses up as Bin Laden, and the Bin Laden figure dances to his music, it doesn't mean he "supports" Bin Laden any more than he "supports" Robin. If he flirts with the possibility of such an interpretation, it is within the context of no subject being taboo to rap. He just sees the world as a vast pool of potential material.

What Eminem is really doing, in a knowing and subtle manner, is toying with a dynamic array of symbols and archetypes. No less knowing, Bin Laden himself also employs archetypes in his videos, using the mythic paraphernalia of

ALEXIS PETRIDIS and GILES FODEN

visionary revelation to motivate his followers and taunt his enemies. It is hardly entertainment, or "popular culture", but the nexus of CNN and the internet can sometimes make it seem so.

On one video, Bin Laden admits the power of September 11 itself as a kind of cultural event, as if the tragedy were nothing but marketing for the release of new product. "Killing oneself for the sake of God was better than the books and pamphlets. They made the whole world listen to them, whether Arab or non-Arab or slaves [using a derogatory slang term for black people] or Chinese. Better than millions of books, tapes or booklets."

Or as Eminem might put it: "Fix your bent antenna, tune it in/ and then I'm gonna/ enter in, endin up under your skin like a splinter/ The centre of attention, back for the winter/ I'm interesting, the best thing since wrestling . . . " GF

EMINEM'S MARTYR COMPLEX

by Gerald Marzorati

from *slate.com*, May 30,2002

remember the culture wars? Those were the '90s conflicts, the ones in which the guys with the beards were gay-rights activists, Hollywood producers, or Robert Bork. Most Americans saw no action in those wars (though they followed them from time to time on talk radio or their cable-news outlet), and so they hardly noticed when the battles drew to a close rather abruptly on Sept. 11. But for a number of cultural warriors, the end of all that back-and-forth about sex and gender, race and teen deviancy, God and PG-13 would seem to have left a hole in their world, a metaphysical Ground Zero. Thus Jerry Falwell's attempt to blame America's alleged moral demise for the collapse of the Twin Towers: What was he trying to do but yell that the culture wars, and *Jerry Falwell*, still mattered? And thus the new CD from Eminem, in which he imagines, or anyway wants *you* to imagine, that America is so terrorized by his rap—post-9/11 and, for that matter, after that schmaltzy Grammy duet with Elton John—that it's hunting *him* down. Welcome, dogs (and Bill Bennett and Tipper, too), to *The Eminem Show*, an album in which what is longed for most is not hot bitches and the violent deaths of Mom and Dad (though they do get theirs) but an America in which a national threat is still somebody who earns a "parental advisory" sticker.

Eminem did have his moment, and not just because he was some sort of outrageous minstrel act—a white boy bursting with lewd boasts and menacing taunts in the nastiest gangsta style. (White suburban kids had been buying lots of rap records, especially gangsta-rap records, for years before Eminem showed up in the late '90s.) He had real talent as a rapper, along with an unschooled writer's gift for assonance and inner rhyme. He was capable of wit—he wasn't just the rap equivalent of Little Johnny's hidden, dogeared porn magazine but of his *Mad* magazine, too. And he was capable of truth, as when, in the song "If I Had" from his first major-label album, *The Slim Shady LP*, he poured out in the hypnotic, list-building cadences of Walt Whitman and Allen Ginsberg the weights and diminishments that could tug down a working-poor kid, even at the height of the so-called Long Boom. (Remember the Long Boom? Educated, grown-up white guys have their own style of outrageous boasting.)

With his new album, though, that mix of social realism and hyperbole—in his hands, an original and combustible compound—has given way to the paranoid delusional. The ranting and the essaying are no longer concerned only or even mostly with the middle-school id of his alter ego, Slim Shady, or with the troubled youth of Marshall Mathers and his issues with class, race, his ex, Kim, his father, and his mother (although the album's only knockout song, "Cleaning Out My Closet," is a howling lament about his mom). Now it's largely about Eminem, the pop star, who seems to have confused celebrity with political and social potency. He would have you believe—he himself wants to believe—that he has such terrifying authority among the young and restless that mainstream America has got to bring him down. Eminem's developed a martyr complex.

In "White America," the album's first song, there is an underground army forming across the nation, kids with bleached hair combed forward, and Eminem is leading them somehow, somewhere, whatever, and Congress is really, really worked up about this. On subsequent tracks, those attempting to shut him up—or worse—include the Bush administration, Lynne Cheney, and the FCC, along with any number of judges, prosecutors, and journalists. As Eminem understands it, he is the national nightmare, the one "everybody just wants to talk about," as he puts it in "Without Me," the first single from the album. That scene in the video for "Without Me"— the one where he dresses up like Osama Bin Laden? It turns out it's *wish fulfillment*.

Actually, the war against al-Qaida does figure briefly in *The Eminem Show*. In a song titled "Square Dance," he warns his troops out there that they soon may be drafted by the Government Man and sent off to die in Afghanistan. Maybe he's been listening to somebody's old Country Joe and the Fish LPs.

One thing he hasn't been listening to closely enough is recent hip-hop. The album's tired beats reinforce the sense that he is stuck in a moment he can't get out of. Dr. Dre, Eminem's producer from the beginning and the one who forged the young rapper's sound, is only a sporadic presence on *The Eminem Show*, which Eminem chose to produce himself. That could explain why the album fails to take account of the surprisingly adventurous atmosphere of mainstream hip-hop,

GERALD MARZORATI

where Timbaland's bhangra-inspired beats propelled last year's best single, Missy Elliot's "Get Ur Freak On," and where the songwriting and production team the Neptunes, when they were not busy making hits for Mystikal, Ludacris, and others, cut a stirring funk-suffused rap record of their own called *In Search Of . . .* that is among this year's finest so far (and still earned that "parental advisory" sticker). Eminem's idea of new and different—or could it be a not quite clever enough allusion to Run DMC's influential rap-rock hit "Walk This Way"?—is to rap about his power and subsequent persecution over Aerosmith's "Dream On."

In the "Without Me" video, not only Bin Laden shows up but Elvis, too, in a bit of nasty bathroom humor—a fat, enfeebled Elvis prepares to die on a toilet at Graceland. Poor Elvis. He had come to believe too early in his career that it wasn't about his songs but about himself—that becoming Elvis, and all that meant, was the whole point, all that anybody cared about, his greatest triumph and truest art. When he has a chance, Eminem might watch that Graceland bit again, as a precaution.

WHITE AMERICAN:

Eminem Makes His Rock Move

by Robert Christgau

from *The Village Voice*, Jun. 11, 2002

the Eminem song of the year is now and will forever remain the Pet Shop Boys' "The Night I Fell in Love," where a certainly fictional, probably underage male spends a night with a performer who tells Stan and Dre jokes and shrugs off those homophobia rumors. In bed, said performer is a nine. Next morning, he "couldn't have been a nicer bloke."

The Eminem moment of the year, however, is where you'd hope it would be, on *The Eminem Show*, rush-released nine days early on Sunday, May 26—UniMoth-Vivendi's defense against downloaders, together with the bonus DVD included in the first two million copies. Unfortunately, the moment isn't situated where you'd hope it would be on the CD itself. Not until the very last of the 15 songs on the 77-minute album (there are also five skits, all but one dead on their feet) does *The Eminem Show* recapture what was so irresistible about Eminem from the first seconds of "My Name Is," with its turf-claiming scratches, catchy-funny chorus, and he-fuck-da-police-in-three-different-voices. "My Name Is" had a spirit that popped up continually and irrepressibly on *The Slim Shady LP* and *The Marshall Mathers LP*: a lightness, a delightedness, a formal mastery whose sense of absolute entitlement never dampens its astonishment that so many CD buyers get the joke.

What's amazing about "My Dad's Gone Crazy" is only secondarily a message. Bottom line, it's a sound. But it's no coincidence that the brashest track on the album sonically is also the deepest thematically. It's the track where Eminem answers the Pet Shop Boys by admitting that he and Dre have been fucking for years. The one where he identifies first with the WTC bombers and then with the bombers' victims. The one where he comes out and explains his aesthetic in terms only a member of Congress or daily rock critic could fail to understand: "My songs can make you cry, take you by surprise at the same time, can make you dry your eyes with the same rhyme/See what you're seeing is a genius at work, which to me isn't work, so it's easy to misinterpret it at first/Cus when I speak, it's tongue-in-cheek, I'd yank my fuckin' teeth before I'd ever bite my tongue." And that's just the beginning.

It's also the one where he admits—a tongue-in-cheek verb for which you may substitute "claims" or "posits" or "pretends"—that "there's no one on earth can save me, not even Hailie." That would be his six-year-old daughter Hailie Jade, joint-custody prize of a 2001 divorce agreement, who on this album represents everything that makes life worth living and sanity worth pursuing. Suitably, crucially, it's Hailie who provides the sonic stroke, a supreme moment among several. She cuts off coke-snorting sounds with a childish "Daddy, what are you doing?" and punctuates a whiny rationalization for homophobia with the older-sounding admonishment "Dad!"; she imitates a chain saw and gets the party started by doubling her father's "OK then, everybody listen up." But most important on an album that proves Eminem's sanity, she utters the words "I think my dad gone crazy" over and over, the perfect take of that phrase looped as a beat. The voice is a child's and yet isn't—overwhelming its little-girl drawl is a guttural gusto that evokes Mercedes McCambridge speaking through Linda Blair, or maybe just the young Brenda Lee. The beat is a celebration, and an exploitation, of Hailie's six-year-old capacity for delight and all the painful experience and threatened entitlement that lurks beyond it. That is the nearest Eminem can come to the 26-year-old amalgam of pain and delight that makes *The Marshall Mathers LP* a stone classic.

I'm not saying *The Eminem Show* isn't a good album. I like it and I enjoy it; I think it represents an articulate, coherent, formally appropriate response to Eminem's changing position and role, one that acknowledges the privileges and alienations that accrue to all fame as well as the resolution of Marshall Mathers's worst traumas and the specifics of his success. It states its business exactly where it should, on the first song, which is one of the good ones: "White America." Some terrific lyrics here. Rather than complaining about his oppression by the media—a wheeze that comes up briefly on only two tracks—he accentuates the positive: "so many motherfuckin' people who feel like me," "a fuckin' army marchin' in back of me." He observes, realistically, that when he was an unknown MC his skin color worked against him, that he was probably as good for Dre's stalled career as Dre was for his potential one. But he also recognizes that at his level of stardom whiteness is an advantage: "Let's do the math, If I was black I would've sold half." Eminem's audience is no longer an expanded version of the hip hop audience. It's bigger and

ROBERT CHRISTGAU

whiter—a "rock" audience. His musical conclusion: to cut back his involvement in the genre he's explored with such brilliance, passion, wit, fidelity, and respect.

There's no such thing as a beat that isn't hip hop—"Walk This Way" proved that long ago. Nevertheless, the music of *The Eminem Show*—12 of its songs produced by Eminem, mostly with longtime beat provider Jeff Bass—owes more to '70s rock than to any strain of black music. Eminem makes no bones about this; in an interview in *The Face*, he asserts it. The rhythms march, stride, and vaunt; they stomp when they're able-bodied and plod when they're lame. The Nate Dogg feature " 'Till I Collapse" is a "We Will Rock You" rip; the one now listed as "Sing for the Moment" used to be called "Dream On," like the old Aerosmith hit it rewrites; for a change, the debut single "Without Me" moves like the most mechanical kind of '70s disco over a simplistic synth hook. Not all of Eminem's grooves are like this; "Cleanin' Out My Closet" and "Soldier" are much jumpier, and "Square Dance," done without Bass, sets Eminem's do-si-do over ominous soundtrack-symphony metal chords, a weird conjunction almost as arresting musically as Hailie's dybbuk voice. Nevertheless, the contrast with the three Dre tracks—which happen to include "My Dad's Gone Crazy"—is pretty stark. The off-kilter shape the Dre beats share, hardly the man's specialty, sticks out in part because it comes as a relief. Especially on the Batman-themed "Business," where among other things Eminem finds a rhyme for "oranges," Dre's funk hints at the lost lightness too often buried underneath the rock self-importance that threatens to sink this album.

Unfortunately, Dre's dull-ass "Hell, yeah"s compromise the effect, a failing that typifies what's saddest about *The Eminem Show*—insofar as it's hip hop, it ain't exactly, how they say it, fresh. It's not funny enough, for one thing. None of the first-rate rhymes are up to the standard of, for example, "The Way

I Am," and although Eminem has never been the "storyteller" lazy defenders pretend he is, the few tracks you could call narratives never think to try for the complexity of "Stan" or "My Fault." Sadder still is that his greatest formal gift—his knack for persona play in which Marshall Mathers, Slim Shady, and Eminem joust over patches of psychic and semiotic territory whose borders no surveyor will ever lay out—only resurfaces with "My Dad's Gone Crazy." When his mom and his ex-wife make their brief appearances, the tone is rock-confessional no matter how extreme or cruel the conceits; the insults leveled at Moby and Jermaine Dupri have no madness in them. Moreover, neither do the much worse insults marshalled at women—"Drips," a vile skank-as-AIDS-carrier vehicle that he shares with his asshole buddies D-12, is even more pro forma than the hackneyed rockboy/rapboy fuck-'em-and-forget-'em of the Dina Rae duet "Superman." It's a depressing testimony to the acuity and diminished expectations of today's sexual discourse that neither of these songs will excite a tenth of the vituperation aimed at "Kim," an agonized working critique of the misogynist mindset both voice so stupidly and regressively.

The self-involved follow-up to a star-time breakthrough is a tale rock has told countless times without enough happy endings, though they certainly happen: *Highway 61 Revisited* and *Rumours* raising, *Fear of a Black Planet* and *In Utero* holding. Maybe we could make *The Slim Shady LP* the breakthrough and *The Marshall Mathers LP* its untoppable culmination. But if it's hope for the future you want, you'll have to seek it out in Eminem's capacity for stupidity and regression. "The Night I Fell in Love" is a great Eminem song because it assumes the standard argument that hip hop's songs of mayhem are "just stories," daring Eminem to take offense at a skillful fable that insults his pathetic manhood while calling him a nice bloke. Where ordinarily the Pet Shop Boys are masters of narrative distance, what's missing in their gibe is persona play—the possibility that the schoolboy protagonist could be Neil Tennant or Chris Lowe. The reason Eminem means more than the Pet Shop Boys at his best is how provocatively and passionately he leaves such questions open, testing the tension between representation and authenticity that's given rock and roll fans that funny feeling in their stomachs for nearly half a century. Because he can be such a jerk, he can also be such a genius. Whether the failure of this album to sell like the last one will drive him to such heights again remains to be heard.

THE EMINEM SHTICK

What Makes a Bigot a Genius? Presiding Over Guilty Pleasures

by Richard Goldstein

from *The Village Voice*, June 12 - 18, 2002

richard wagner was a great artist, but he was also an anti-Semite, and most assessments of his genius address this fact. *The Birth of a Nation* is a great film, but no appreciation can ignore its racism. No one dismisses such discussions as politically correct. But when it comes to art that is profoundly, even violently, sexist or homophobic, a different standard applies. Any attempt to confront the social meaning of such work is met with stiff—and I do mean stiff—resistance. Many men consider it their right to enjoy sexual bigotry, and many women want in on the action.

The latest example of identifying with the aggressor is the largely idolatrous reaction to Eminem's new album. Hip critics quibble that he's fallen off his edge—as would anyone but a genuine genius, given the speed with which outrage becomes shtick in pop culture. The usual response to Eminem's situation is to up the ante by being even nastier, but bitch slapping and fag bashing have been declared off-limits for the duration of the war on terror. The record industry has been reduced to saluting the flag and honoring bluegrass. What's a celebrity bigot to do?

The answer, for Eminem, is to carve a canny path down the middle. The sexual violence is more muted, though not absent from his new collection (that would be like leaving the dyke scene out of a porno). But it's contextualized by what trial lawyers call "the abuse excuse." Under the basher lies a boy betrayed by his wife and his mother. We've heard it all before, just as we've seen Eminem walk the line between talking the talk and deconstructing it. But repetition is an important part of brand building. So welcome to **The Eminem Show**, the pomo equivalent of Louis Armstrong singing "Hello, Dolly." It's so nice to have him back where he belongs.

> *I never would've dreamed in a million years I'd see*
> *So many motherfuckin people who feel like me*
> *Who share the same views and the same exact beliefs*
> *It's like a fuckin army marchin in back of me*

By now, these legions include not just middle-class white kids but middle-aged *machers* who measure their years in the distance from weed to equities. One of them, a family man named Paul Slansky, wrote an homage to Eminem in a recent issue of *The New York Observer*. Watching him perform at the Grammys, "I fell in love," Slansky gushed (hastening to add, "not *that* way, dawg"). Confessing to this crush, he discovers that his fine-dining friends all feel the same way. It seems there's a secret order of dawgs *moyens sensuels*, and Slansky wants them to come out proud. "There should be no stigma attached to being an Adult Who Loves Eminem," he writes.

The notion that there's something courageous about this attraction has been carefully cultivated; it's a classic marketing strategy. But in fact, Eminem's ascension is a glaring example of the herd reflex passing for rebellion. The real dissenters are the activists who've been pummeled for failing to see the complexity and originality of this bleach-blond Baudelaire. As a former rock critic, I know how easy it is to throw the word *genius* around. In this case, however, it's not about a lack of standards. It's about using the imprimatur of art to avoid looking your pleasure in the eye.

The aesthetic defense is one of many Eminem alibis. We've been assured that this is just a pop-art pose, a cry from the working-class streets, an act of defiance against the forces of censorship, a repository for feelings we can't express in life, an exorcism of our demons, or a sex charade. Of course, the same thing could be said about racist or anti-Semitic entertainment. Imagine a performer rapping, "I'll stab you in the head/Whether you're a kike or yid/Hate hebes? The answer's yes." I don't think a critic like Janet Maslin would respond as she has to Eminem: "A lot of what he says makes me uncomfortable, but the bottom line is if it's good, you have to acknowledge that, and it is. It's very cathartic to listen to him."

Say what you will about redeeming social (or artistic) value: At its hard core, Eminem's poetics is pornography, and it's accorded the same privileges. Just as we've declared the XXX zone exempt from social thinking, we refuse to subject sexist rap to moral scrutiny. We crave a space free from the demands of equity, especially when it comes to women, whose rise has inspired much more ambivalence than most men are willing to admit. This is especially true in the middle class, where feminism has made its greatest impact. No wonder Eminem is so

NOISE

hot to suburban kids and Downtown *alter cockers*. He's as nasty as they wanna be.

Once you call this stuff cathartic, it's a small step to removing it from the world entirely. Eminem's music becomes an encapsulated experience, all the more heavily defended because it's a guilty pleasure. Rock titans like Dylan and Lennon inspired a very different reaction, because their songs related to the rest of life. But the hermetic quality of pornopop makes it float above meaning. You can imagine anything you like about this sadistic spectacle, including a masochistic response.

A lot of hip people are consoled by the Pet Shop Boys' funky homage to Eminem, in which he gets turned on by a gay boy and turns out to be a tender lover. In the academy, this is called appropriation—the queer corollary to those earthy essays by post-feminists who like to pig out to misogynistic ditties. Presumably they're in no danger of hooking up with a B-boy, unlike the girls learning to eroticize guys who call them bitches. I wonder how Slansky would feel about a daughter of his having such a mate. But I'm not about to argue that children should be protected from this music—or that they can be. The danger isn't the fantasies Eminem generates but the refusal to see them as anything more than that.

There *is* a relationship between Eminem and his time. His bigotry isn't incidental or stupid, as his progressive champions claim. It's central and knowing—and unless it's examined, it will be free to operate. Not that this music makes men rape any more than the Klan-lionizing imagery in *Birth of a Nation* creates racists. The real effect is less personal than systematic. Why is it considered proper to speak out against racism and anti-Semitism but not against sexism and homophobia? To me, this disparity means we haven't reached a true consensus about these last two biases. We aren't ready to let go of male supremacy. We still think something central to the universe will be lost if this arrangement changes.

What is the relationship between that anxiety and the rise of Eminem? That's a question criticism must confront. It's not enough to repudiate his sexism in passing. That's a disclaimer, not an interrogation. It skirts the crucial issue of why this stuff is so hot. And it presumes that we're drawn to rapine rap *despite* its sexual violence. That's the most dangerous form of denial.

NOISE

GUESS WHO THINKS EMINEM'S A GENIUS?
MIDDLE-AGED ME

by Paul Slansky

from **The New York Observer**,
June 3, 2002

if you're anything like me, you're middle-aged, you have a fabulous wife and kid, you see a shrink, you really should lose 15 pounds, you think Albert Brooks is funny and Billy Crystal is not, and you can't believe that anyone can look at this nasty little prick Bush and see a "President." And …

And sometime in the past couple of years, you had your Eminem moment. Maybe it was on the 2000 MTV Video Music Awards when he sang "Will the real Slim Shady please stand up?" while leading a swarm of look-alikes into Radio City Music Hall. Maybe, as in my case, it was his performance of "Stan" with Elton John on the 2001 Grammys. Or maybe, as it occurred with more than a dozen of my friends, someone who'd just found him turned you on to what you'd been missing.

Whatever. Chances are that you're a little uneasy about your Eminem enthusiasm and that you don't share this guilty pleasure indiscriminately, lest someone who still dismisses him as an obscene lout will think you insane.

You're not. For the rock 'n' roll generation, Eminem, né Marshall Mathers III, is the most compelling figure to have emerged from popular music since the holy trinity of Dylan, Lennon and Jagger. There should be no stigma attached to being an Adult Who Loves Eminem. Besides, as my sitcom-writing friend Danny Zuker said, "We're actually the perfect fans for him, because we're the least likely to shoot up a school after listening to him."

As the man himself points out in his infectious new hit, "Without Me," the airwaves have indeed felt empty without him. But the wait is over and the results are as thrilling as they are unsettling. *The Eminem Show* (Interscope) is Eminem's third great album in 40 months — an astonishing output comparable to the peak creative bursts of the Beatles, the Stones and Dylan — and the only one you'll need to get through the summer.

Statistically speaking, this album should have been a disappointment. Right now, Eminem's the biggest star in music, his first movie (the Curtis Hanson–directed *8 Mile*, about an Eminem-like white rapper) is slated to be released in November, and he's got more money than all of his ancestors put together had in their whole lives. History tells us that all of these should be working like opiates on Eminem, dulling his rage and his wit and his connection to the griminess of real life.

But the great thing — for us, if not for him — is that, despite all of his good fortune, Eminem is still pissed off. His greatest joy — besides his daughter Hailie Jade — is his ability, as he says on the new album, to get "under your skin like a splinter."

Eminem, with his ego so big it needs two alters, has three singers in his band. In "Without Me," nasal-voiced Slim Shady boasts about his return to save music from terminal blandness. "Now let's go, give me the signal / I'll be there with a whole list full of new insults," he raps. And the song, with its retro-disco beat, slinky sax and hilariously self-aware lyrics, actually does come to the rescue, creating something you're actually excited to hear on the radio.

Then there's "White America," the pounding punk/metal anthem that blasts open the album. Eminem takes the lead on this one, a thundering rant defending freedom of speech, and what more fun way to do that than to shout about burning the flag and pissing on the White House lawn, and, oh, "Fuck you, Ms. Cheney"?

It's not Eminem's fault that the post-Vietnam, post-Watergate culture he grew up with was such a moral sewer of cynicism, sensationalism and exploitation that he now has to ratchet up the outrageousness to Grand Guignol levels to get us to pay attention.

Referring to the F.C.C.'s recently aborted effort to fine a radio station for playing his music, Eminem gloats, "And now they're sayin' I'm in trouble with the government, I'm lovin' it, I shoveled shit all my life / and now I'm dumping it!" Great rock stars have been pushing the envelope for 50 years now, but I can't recall anyone with Eminem's popularity getting more of a kick out of giving the world the finger.

"I love pissin' you off," he says on "Soldier," "it gets me off, like my lawyers, when the fuckin' judge lets me off." And it amazes him how effortless it is. "Don't you people see I'm just saying shit to fucking get a rise out of you?" he said a while back. "You're letting me win!"

NOISE

But "White America" is more than just a verbal Molotov cocktail. The song is also an astute self-assessment of who Eminem is in the culture, how he got there, who his fans are, and why he's a threat: "See the problem is I speak to suburban kids who otherwise woulda never knew these words exist / whose moms probably woulda never gave two squirts of piss, till I created so much motherfuckin' turbulence / straight out the tube, right into your living rooms I came, and kids flipped when they knew I was produced by Dre / That's all it took, and they were instantly hooked right in, and they connected with me too because I looked like them."

Critics who complain about Eminem's relentless self-obsession are missing the point. Translating what it's like to be him into the metaphors he can communicate to the world is exactly where the art comes in. The more personal he makes his work, the more universal it becomes. Because he's so damned interesting to himself, he becomes interesting to us.

"Most people, you ask them what's going on in their life and they say, 'Oh, nothing much,'" said writer Steve Radlauer. "And they mean it. Eminem can't believe how much is going on in his life, he's reveling in the details, like a great political writer analyzing a great election, or Calvin Trillin writing about parking a car in Manhattan. It's a great sociological work-in-progress."

There is, in this new album, a subtle effort to reposition himself as more of a soldier in the culture wars, and less of a misogynistic, homophobic wack job. It's not entirely successful – his seeming hatred for the entire female gender, save for his daughter, can be hard to take – but still, he's trying.

Eminem's first album featured the song "97' Bonnie & Clyde," about taking his baby daughter along on an errand to dump her mother's body in a lake. The second album had the prequel, "Kim," as harrowing a blast of murderous rage — "Now bleed! Bitch, bleed!" — as pop music has produced. Its intensity made the Stones' "Midnight Rambler" sound like a poseur's nursery rhyme. Even Eminem, who sports a tattoo on his stomach that's addressed to his ex-wife — "KIM R.I.P. (ROT IN PIECES)" — has said he doesn't listen to it anymore. On the new album, there's no song about killing Kim, though there are a few references to coming close.

There's such a variety of musical genres and such a barrage of verbiage on *The Eminem Show* that it will take weeks to absorb it all. My current choice for funniest line is this depiction in "Superman" of a post-coital moment with a groupie: "First thing you say, 'I'm not fazed, I hang around big stars all day / I don't see what the big deal is anyway, you're just plain old Marshall to me' / Oooh yeah girl run that game, 'Hailie Jade, I love that name / Love that tattoo, what's that say? "Rot In Pieces," uh, that's great.'"

"There's so much 'meta' in Eminem," said writer Fred Schruers. "He's always examining the reception he's getting." As he sings on "Without Me," "Feel the tension soon as someone mentions me."

The best song on the album is "Cleanin' Out My Closet." The real Marshall Mathers sings this one, and the track's deceptively pretty melody and chorus — "I'm sorry, Mama, I never meant to hurt you" — provides the counterpoint to the artist's ultimate fuck-you to the inadequate mother whose refusal to "admit you was wrong" keeps his rage white-hot.

"And Hailie's getting so big now, you should see her, she's beautiful / But you'll never see her, she won't even be at your funeral," he sings. "How dare you try to take what you didn't help me to get / You selfish bitch, I hope you fuckin' burn in hell for this shit / Remember when Ronnie died and you said you wished it was me? / Well, guess what, I am dead. Dead to you as can be."

NOISE

Whew!

On an up note, the same song recounts the June 2000 incident in which Eminem was arrested for pistol-whipping a guy he caught kissing his wife outside a Detroit nightclub. Occurring as it did mere days after his last CD, *The Marshall Mathers LP*, set first-week sales records on its way to going octuple platinum, the episode appeared to be one of those self-destructive acts that an angry man might commit in the wake of phenomenal success, but on "Cleanin' Out My Closet," Marshall, who was sentenced to two years of probation as a result of the encounter, reveals a nascent ability to protect himself from himself: "What I did was stupid, no doubt it was dumb / but the smartest shit I did was take the bullets out of that gun / Cuz I'da killed 'em, shit I would have shot Kim an' him both / It's my life, I'd like to welcome y'all to The Eminem Show."

As he sings on "Superman," Eminem isn't interested in being a man of steel. Our best artists are never perfect people, and so we must deal with the duality — or in Eminem's case, the plurality — of personae. Yes, he's a misogynist, *and* he has valid things to say. You know, like O.J. is guilty *and* there are corrupt cops.

The culture police would have us believe that Eminem is telling kids, "Take drugs, drive drunk, kill, rape, maim," but actual listening reveals a far more moral, almost poignant, message: Parents, do your goddamn job.

As he says in "Who Knew": "Don't blame me when li'l Eric jumps off of the terrace / You shoulda been watchin' him — apparently you ain't parents."

Granted, he's not doing anything to make our jobs easier, but he'd say that he raised himself, he helped raise his half-brother Nathan, he's raising Hailie Jade. Our kids are not his concern.

So, how did we aging boomers find him? While my wife Liz and I pride ourselves on having kept up with music into middle age, the birth of our daughter Grace in 1998 reduced our listening hours drastically. We wallowed in parenthood, blissfully oblivious to Eminem's march on pop culture. After three years of *Teletubbies* and *Barney* and *Blue's Clues*, we were craving something with a bit more edge.

And then, there it was, on the Grammys, of all places: Eminem performing "Stan." "Dear Slim, I wrote you but you still ain't callin' / I left my cell, my pager, and my home phone at the bottom / I sent two letters back in autumn / You must not have got 'em..."

The combination of the song itself — has there ever been, in any medium, a truer portrait of a deranged fan? — and the intensity of Eminem's delivery was revelatory. I fell instantly in love like I had only once before, on the Saturday afternoon in 1964 when I first saw the Rolling Stones, on WPIX's *Clay Cole Show*.

I bought both of his CDs the next day and drove around all afternoon immersed in the giddy experience of being completely entertained. *The Marshall Mathers LP* dazzled with its brilliant five-song exegesis on celebrity — "Kill You," "Stan," "Who Knew," "The Way I Am" and "The Real Slim Shady" — that may be the greatest kickoff of any album ever. But its predecessor, *The Slim Shady LP*, was equally impressive in the way it showed how the numbing pain of poverty — "That's rock bottom / When you feel like you've had it up to here / 'Cause you mad enough to scream but you sad enough to tear" — leads inevitably to a certain nihilism: "If I had one wish / I would ask for a big enough ass for the whole world to kiss."

NOISE

By nightfall I was on the phone proselytizing about this great new thing I'd discovered two years late. My friend Mr. Zuker, a father of three, was relieved. "I'm so glad to hear this," he said, "because I've been driving around listening to Eminem for months now, and I thought I was having my midlife crisis."

Within days I'd tracked down a half dozen bootlegs compiling all of the guest raps, soundtrack contributions and independent label releases that made up the rest of his output. On an obscure track called "Any Man," I found this rhyme: "I strike a still pose and hit you with some ill flows / That don't even make sense, like dykes using dildos."

The song ended: "Somethin', somethin', somethin', somethin' I get weeded / My daughter scribbled over that rhyme, I couldn't read it."

Given the precious little that most people bring to their celebrity status, Eminem's talents are enormous. Start with the writing: the attention to detail, the musician's ear for the rhythms of exactly how people talk, the way it can take you by surprise and make you laugh out loud, often at something horrific, as when the self-loathing star mocks the notion of being anyone's role model: "I got genital warts and it burns when I pee / Don't you wanna grow up to be just like me? / I'll tie a rope around my penis and jump from a tree / You probably wanna grow up to be just like me!!!"

Beyond the words are the beats. Being so closely identified with Dr. Dre, the Phil Spector of hip-hop, Eminem's own natural musicality has been hugely underrated. On *The Eminem Show*, Dre produced three tracks. Eminem produced or co-produced 12, and the album sounds great.

And beyond his talent are his balls. His stuff was political, if not politically correct, from the start, because his main subject was poverty and what's more political than that? But the mini-Armageddons that officially ushered in the new millennium have blown us back to the late '60s: The country is "at war," whatever that means, and a kid — as well as that kid's parents — would have to be stupid to assume that the administration couldn't resume the draft, like, yesterday if they wanted to. Someone has to remind everyone that we still have freedom of speech here, that it's the bedrock of everything else the country claims to be and to stand for, and that questioning the government — or using profanity — is not unpatriotic.

And here that someone is, spitting contempt for those elders so undeserving of respect, declaring himself, as he does in "Square Dance," not just willing but eager to "ambush this Bush administration, mush the Senate's face in, push this generation / of kids to stand and fight for the right to say something you might not like."

Who was this Marshall Mathers III? How was it that this guy who had probably listened to very little, if any, Dylan seemed to be channeling the same absurdist/protest muses?

An hour on the Web filled in the blanks: Born to 17-year-old mom, Debbie, in 1972. Instantly abandoned by dad, Marshall Mathers II. Spent childhood ping-ponging between Kansas City and Detroit with mom and her mood swings. Always the new kid in school, always getting beaten up. After a particularly rough encounter, wound up comatose.

Best friend was mom's teenage brother, Uncle Ronnie, whose not inconsiderable contribution to the world, before committing suicide, was turning Marshall on to rap.

Had extremely volatile relationship with girlfriend Kim (whom he eventually married and soon divorced), the mother of his beloved 6-year-old Hailie Jade. Was going nowhere in rap when, while taking a shit, thought up "Slim Shady," the droog-like doppelgänger who could do all the venting and spewing he clearly needed to do. Got signed by Dre, video for "My Name Is" aired round the clock on MTV. Sold 4 million copies of first album. Got sued for $10 million by mom upset about being portrayed as a pillhead whose chief pastimes were Bingo and lawsuits. (She settled for $25,000.) Replaced the ridiculous and essentially harmless Marilyn Manson as music's Public Enemy No. 1, uniting left (GLAAD) and right (Lynne Cheney) in a crusade to shut him the fuck up.

I started pushing Eminem on friends. "Unbelievable!" e-mailed the poet Marilyn Johnson, married 16 years with three kids. "He is making art."

"I thought he was a punk asshole and I never thought in a bazillion years I'd listen to his music," said *Los Angeles Times* copy editor Matt Coltrin, "but now I can't stop." Even writer Jerry Lazar, whose favorite Beatle had always been Paul, was impressed, once he "stopped listening with parent ears" and could hear things besides "bitch" and "fuck."

Resistance was futile. "I can't afford to think he's brilliant," said the mother of two teenage girls. A week later her husband called to say, "Thanks so much for the Eminem. We drove from L.A. up to San Francisco and listened to him the whole way."

New York Times critic Janet Maslin, who likes Eminem more than either of her teenage sons do, met him on the Detroit set of *8 Mile* last winter and described him as "serious, articulate and not at all overbearing" during their interview. "He was interested to talk about acting, because it was new for him. He didn't mind that he had a lot to learn, but he was going to learn it his own way."

Ms. Maslin said that her fandom "does not come without guilt. A lot of what he says makes me uncomfortable, but the bottom line is if it's good, you have to acknowledge that, and it is. It's very cathartic to listen to him, it's like Quentin Tarantino's best stuff, there's an energy to it."

My wife, whose first angry young man of music was Elvis

Costello, thinks we middle-aged fans are responding to Eminem's ability to give voice to the rage that we can no longer express so freely now that we have to do things like drive car pool, so we drop the kids off at school, roll down the windows, and blast "The Way I Am" on the ride home.

Or maybe it's that music makes its imprint on you at whatever age you first hear it and, throughout your life, evokes that age when you hear it again. If you were branded by "(I Can't Get No) Satisfaction" when you were 15, you're going to feel 15 again when you hear "White America," and how many drugs can do that?

If you've read this far, I have to believe you're already a fan, but if not — if you've let Lynne Cheney and GLAAD define Eminem for you — you have to make up your own mind. Go buy the new CD. In fact, get all three. It'll save you a trip back to the store tomorrow.

PAUL SLANSKY

NOISE

SYMPATHY FOR THE DEVIL

by Kelefa Sanneh

from *The New Yorker*,
June 24, 2002

On May 23, 2000, Eminem released the last great album of the twentieth century. His previous two albums had proved him to be a clever and foulmouthed rapper, but "The Marshall Mathers LP" was his masterpiece, condensing a few years of American culture into seventy-two minutes of tasteless jokes about Bill Clinton and "South Park," Jennifer Lopez and Christopher Reeve, Gianni Versace's murder and the Columbine massacre. There was a series of jabs at Britney Spears, Christina Aguilera, Will Smith, and *NSYNC, which was Eminem's way of acknowledging that they all inhabited the exuberant universe of "Total Request Live," the MTV program that screened their music videos back to back before a studio audience of screaming teen-agers. The best part was that Eminem knew his place in this world. He knew that he owed his career to the celebrity industry, knew that his tabloid sensibility was well suited to a tabloid culture, knew that the whole enterprise was built on bad faith. "Became a commodity 'cause I'm W-H-I-T-E / 'Cause MTV was so friendly to me," he rapped-and he wasn't really complaining.

Two years later, tabloid culture isn't what it used to be, and MTV executives are scrambling to keep "Total Request Live" from slipping in the ratings. Eminem's new album, "The Eminem Show" (Aftermath/Interscope), includes a few digs at mainstream stars, but his foes seem diminished, and so does he. He picks a fight with Moby, the mild-mannered electronica producer, calling him a "thirty-six-year-old baldheaded fag," and telling him, "It's over-nobody listens to techno." (Moby posted a polite response on his Web site: "Eminem has skills as an mc, but it disturbs me that he glorifies homophobia and misogyny in his songs.") He threatens to beat up Chris Kirkpatrick, from *NSYNC, which reveals merely that Eminem is the rare twenty-nine-year-old man who can still name the members of an aging boy band. He has to comment on the attacks of September 11th, so he compares himself to the terrorists—"There's no plane that I can't learn how to fly." If Eminem wants to remain Public Enemy No. 1, he'll have to do better than that.

Luckily, the rapper has found a new victim, someone who can give as good as he gets: himself. On earlier albums, he turned his life into a cartoon, starring "regular guy" Marshall Mathers (Eminem's real name) and his "crazy" alter ego, Slim Shady; he even created an animated series called "The Slim Shady Show." Now he seems to be trying to turn the cartoon into a life. The booklet accompanying the CD is filled with photographs that look like surveillance footage, complete with date and time: we see him taking out the trash, writing rhymes at his kitchen table, and even, on the front cover, behind a stage curtain, ready to step up to a microphone. It's his show, and he's playing all the roles: persecuted celebrity, eager star, shrewd producer.

Some of these characters are familiar; previous albums introduced us to Eminem's mother, Debbie, and his wife, Kim. ("The Marshall Mathers LP" included a brutal homicidal fantasy about her.) Now he brags about his divorce from Kim and attempts to settle the score with his mother by offering incriminating details about his childhood. ("I was made to believe I was sick when I wasn't!" he tells us.) He also tries out a new role: caring father. In "Hailie's Song," a song for his six-year-old daughter, he says, "I feel like singing," and that's what he does, crooning (and sometimes screaming) a stirring ballad about fatherly love: "My baby girl keeps getting older, I watch her grow up with pride." Later, on "My Dad's Gone Crazy," he brags about his "brains, brawn, and brass balls," while Hailie giggles, "You're funny, Daddy."

Because he's a white rapper, Eminem has been lumped in with the rock-rap movement, but he has generally shied away from the music. While Kid Rock, another white rapper from Detroit, crossed over to rock and roll and country music, Eminem worked to establish hip-hop bona fides, taking his musical cues from Dr. Dre, a hip-hop classicist who still believes in bass lines and backbeats, and who became his mentor and producer.

But the new album represents a change of course; rock and roll is everywhere. Eminem has said, "I was trying to capture, like, a seventies rock vibe." He produced or co-produced nearly all the songs; Dr. Dre produced just three. Where Dr. Dre's style was tuneful and sprightly (he loves pizzicato), Eminem writes in the key of strife, gravitating toward minor-key melodies that evoke hard-rock bands such as Korn, and he delivers many of his lyrics in a nasal yell. "Cleanin Out My Closet" pairs a wailed chorus with an electric guitar, and

"'Till I Collapse" borrows the familiar rhythm from "We Will Rock You," by Queen. On "Sing for the Moment," an attempt to explain why fans feel so strongly about him, Eminem samples a chorus (and a guitar solo) from Aerosmith's 1973 song "Dream On." He describes one young listener "walking around with his headphones blaring, alone in his own zone":

> His thoughts are wacked, he's mad, so he's talking back,
> Talking black, brainwashed from rock and rap
> He sags his pants, do-rags and a stocking cap
> His stepfather hit him, so he socked him back.

This album is a private show, a sullen CD designed to be heard through headphones, and guaranteed to appeal to zoned-out white kids who start "talking black" when they get mad.

Most hip-hop, though, is social music, not headphone music-rappers like to imagine their songs shaking night-club floors or booming out of cars. The doctrine of hip-hop triumphalism is inherently inclusive; it proceeds from the assumption that everyone already loves the music. That assumption was what made "The Marshall Mathers LP" so creepy. The tone was conspiratorial, not confrontational: Eminem figured that his listeners were having as much fun as he was. He won us over with jokes, enthralled us with stories, disarmed us with his passion for language. Even his homophobic slurs were unleashed with a wink and a nudge. His words would "stab you in the head, whether you're a fag or les," he said, but the threat quickly dissolved into wordplay: "or the homo-sex, hermaph or a trans-a-ves, pants or dress." He has always understood the sophisticated pleasures of complicity. You succumbed to his charms with a sigh and, perhaps, a few reservations-the way you succumbed to Britney Spears, or *NSYNC, or, for that matter, Bill Clinton.

"The Eminem Show" is more self-righteous, more vehement, and more paranoid, which may just mean that it's more rock and roll. Instead of saying indefensible things and trusting that we will love him anyway, Eminem explains his hardships and pleads his case, which is a very rock-and-roll thing to do-rappers don't usually beg for sympathy. Hip-hop triumphalism has given way to grungy defeatism, and it's difficult not to think of Kurt Cobain when Eminem says, "I'm trapped, if I could go back, I never would have rapped / I sold my soul to the devil, I'll never get it back." We're not Eminem's co-defendants anymore; we're the jury, summoned to pass judgment on yesterday's crimes.

By any standard, "The Eminem Show" is an impressive achievement, smart and passionate and hummable. And it may be just the right album for the current moment, in which the sleazy patter of hip-hop and tabloid culture has given way to the jittery onslaughts of rock and roll and terrorism. Like his listeners, Eminem is living in a changed world, and although he has adapted gracefully, there's a hint of melancholy. The new decade may have brought him clarity, but it came at a price: the music he's making is more conventional, less concerned with rants and jokes than with feelings. There's less wordplay and less glee. A few years ago, it was easy to disparage the decadent culture that produced "The Marshall Mathers LP." Now that we've seen the alternative, perhaps we should reconsider. Is it too early to be nostalgic for 1999?

KELEFA SANNEH

NOISE

BUT CAN HE ACT?

by Geoff Boucher

from *Los Angeles Times*,
October 13, 2002

They ushered the Detroit kid into the Hollywood chamber of power and sat him down on a crimson couch beneath perfectly framed photographs of grinning movie stars. They told him he, too, could be a star and waited for him to be giddy or nervous or even visibly interested. Instead, the kid shrugged and said, "Yeah, OK."

That was in January 2000, when Eminem was a music sensation but not yet assured the twin titles of world's top rapper and American pop culture's most incendiary young artist. His music and videos were theatrical, but there was really no reason to believe he could carry a movie. And it was arguably ludicrous to assume he could shoulder a gritty drama written, directed and filmed by people with exactly zero background in the rap world. Somehow, though, that is exactly what happened.

The bold result, a film called "8 Mile," should make

Eminem a cultural force of newfound potency and, just maybe, put him in a place where he won't have to explain himself anymore.

"8 Mile," which opens Nov. 8, has in Eminem a star who has been a cannonball in the pool of pop music, hailed by some as a Lenny Bruce of street music and reviled by others as just another rusty nail on the cultural landscape. It also has 57-year-old director Curtis Hanson, who was praised for the confident craft of "L.A. Confidential" and "Wonder Boys" but came to "8 Mile" with a creeping worry that he might be a clumsy tourist in rap. Its screenwriter, meanwhile, is the man who co-wrote and directed the 1999 film "The Mod Squad," a failure so bruising that, when asked what in "8 Mile" most reflects his voice, he cited the scene where the main character vomits backstage because he is so afraid of his audience.

The trajectory of the "8 Mile" project was set by the fame of Eminem, which could have sent the movie in one of two directions—either a commercial-minded farce with a hit soundtrack or a film that uses its built-in allure to take some chances. The course it took, which started two years ago in the office of producer Brian Grazer, is clearly the latter, and that makes "8 Mile" the most intriguing music-star film in years.

"I remember he was sitting here and he would not look at me, he would only look straight ahead," recalls Grazer, whose movie, "A Beautiful Mind," won the Oscar for best picture of 2001. "When you bring people in, at least they usually look at you or at least eventually talk. He just didn't."

Grazer had set the meeting after catching a glimpse of Eminem on an MTV awards show. The producer had for years been meeting rappers, from Slick Rick to Tone Loc, looking for a star for a "meaningful" hip-hop film, the one who could do for hip-hop youth what "Blackboard Jungle" had done for rock 'n' roll kids and "Saturday Night Fever" for disco kids.

Why did Grazer think the unblinking white kid on his couch was the one? Especially considering Eminem has been excoriated for lyrics of venom, homophobia, violence and lewdness? "I never had any doubt," Grazer says. "Just seeing him on TV for six seconds I knew he could act. And then when he came here and I was with him, I couldn't keep my eyes off him. . . . And this movie is going to change the way a lot of people look at him."

The success of the film awaits the critics and box office, but screenings at the Toronto International Film Festival and a Puerto Rico convention of hip-hop DJs have created positive buzz. If it does succeed, "8 Mile" will be an unlikely bridge between Hollywood and Detroit that also illuminates on film how issues of race are bending to the backbeat of hip-hop.

Not quite a biography

"**8** Mile" is not the life story of its star, but it flirts so closely with the path of young Marshall Bruce Mathers III to his stardom as Eminem that the movie feels like a rap remix—tweaked but with the same beats. The movie follows one week in the life of Jimmy "Rabbit" Smith who, at the start of the film, is forced to move into a trailer with his boozy mother. The film's title is the roadway that separates that trailer in the poor, white rural community from the poor, urban black areas where Rabbit finds the comfort of hip-hop culture. Rabbit is an outsider on both sides of 8 Mile.

For Hanson, the film is as much about geography as biography, a map of Detroit's despairs. The director spent time in the city in the 1980s researching a project on child drug dealers and, when he saw the "8 Mile" script written by Scott Silver, he remembered how young Detroiters seemed like kids at play in a condemned factory.

GEOFF BOUCHER

A number of top directors vied for "8 Mile," but Grazer says he tapped Hanson because he "is an American director who can tell an American story, and that's what this is." Hanson was blunt, though, when he went to Detroit to meet Eminem: He would sign on if the star committed to a serious youth film, a "Rebel Without a Cause," not a two-hour music video.

"That's where our bond started," Hanson recalls. "He saw that I was going to demand of him a performance that felt sufficiently and emotionally true to carry a movie without the crutch of the hit tunes, a high bar for someone their first time out."

The script had been written by Silver, who was coming off "The Mod Squad" but was able to win over Grazer's people with a script he had written about Richard Pryor. Once hired, Silver, who describes himself as a 38-year-old white guy from Malibu, went out and bought $700 in rap CDs. More educational were grainy videos of Eminem in 1990s rap "battles," the swaggering rhyme competitions that trace back to rap's 1970s birth in New York. The battles would become the signature scenes in "8 Mile" and make for the moments of music-as-urban-escape that propelled "Saturday Night Fever," "Flashdance" and "Purple Rain."

Silver's script was flexible as far as setting, but Hanson was resolute that Detroit be the locale for the story and all filming. In "Wonder Boys," Hanson used the bridges of Pittsburgh to convey the film's life passages and in "8 Mile," he wanted Detroit to be the harsh sidewalk that can't stifle the weeds of youth and art. To capture the grit, the director tapped cinematographer Rodrigro Prieto, who surveyed Mexico's mean streets in "Amores Perros," and Philip Messina, production designer for the narcotics epic "Traffic." He also cast locals as rappers, factory workers and even as Rabbit's sister. The more difficult task, however, was preparing the novice Eminem. Six weeks of rehearsal were scheduled, much of them in a Detroit riverfront hotel with auditioning actors in an exercise to hone the rapper's nascent craft.

For emotional compass points, Hanson showed Eminem "Raging Bull" and "Romper Stomper," the Australian film of violent youth, as well as "Killer of Sheep," Charles Burnett's 1977 gem about Watts street life. Eminem "soaked everything up like a sponge," Hanson says.

And the sponge felt wrung out by the process. "Working with Curtis was like going into film boot camp," Eminem says. "It was long, grueling and difficult. But I think the end product speaks for itself."

If Hanson educated Eminem in film, the rapper made the director a rap fan of nuance. "The New York way of saying 'yo' is different than the Detroit 'yo'—it comes in the sentence in an entirely different place. Did you know that?" Hanson also recognized the advantage of setting "8 Mile" in 1995 when the East Coast vs. West Coast rivalry was still fought with words. The characters reference the rivalry in the way rock fans used to debate Stones vs. Beatles. "There was a sort of innocence still," he says.

The pair huddled often to plan Rabbit's battle rhymes, and Hanson noted Eminem's ability to consume information and return it in clever and dizzying ways. In his downtime, the rapper hunched over a notebook, scrawling lyrics. Hanson could hear Eminem's music seeping through the dressing room walls as the rapper toiled on a new recording for the final scene. The finished product, "Lose Yourself," is Eminem's latest radio hit.

"Has there ever been a movie where the star wrote the song on the set and recorded it for the movie's ending?" Hanson asks. "It's like everything was heading toward that song, the character ends up in that place."

You better lose yourself in the music
The moment you own it you better never let it go, oh

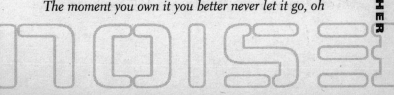

You only get one shot, do not miss your chance to blow
Cuz opportunity comes once in a lifetime, yo

— "Lose Yourself"

No more 'white culture'?

The song "Lose Yourself" is pumping out of the stereo speakers on the balcony of Jimmy Iovine's Santa Monica office as the music mogul calls an assistant to track down "American Skin." Iovine says the new book by Leon E. Wynter and its race analysis resonate in "8 Mile."

"American Skin" says the nation's melting pot is now on high simmer because of cultural forces, among them the brawn of rap in art and commerce. The book predicts "white culture" will soon be as meaningful to young people as a typewriter repair manual. Iovine, co-chairman of Interscope Records—the label for Eminem's three albums—and an executive producer of "8 Mile," wanted to see that on film.

Eminem's ascension began in earnest when an Interscope intern handed Iovine an amateur recording of the Detroit rhymer and Iovine passed it on to Dr. Dre. Iovine knows that this new chapter in Eminem's career will only enhance the rapper's value to Interscope (career artists and multimedia stars are desperately sought tonic in the ailing music industry) but he says "8 Mile" also has cultural insight.

Rappers have become movie stars, but rap in film is most often a soundtrack for urban comedy and crime. "8 Mile" seeks rap truth, Iovine says. "The power of hip-hop is in these race changes, and you see these changes beginning in the 1990s with the kids in this movie," Iovine says. "It's about class, not race, and hip-hop is one of the reasons."

Rabbit is well aware of race and class in "8 Mile." In a clever word concoction, Rabbit's crew is called Three-One-Third.

The reference is to Detroit's 313 area code but also to the crew's membership: Three blacks and Rabbit, who is the one-third—it's a sly joke on the 19th century legal view that blacks counted as "one-third" of a white person. In late 20th century Detroit, Rabbit is the fraction.

"The whole film made me strip my ego back down to the guy I was in '95," Eminem says. "Everything from the schooling in acting to the broke world that Jimmy lived in was strange. It brought me back to actually feeling like the guy I was."

When Rabbit finally wins over the black crowd at the Shelter club battles, it's by showing that he is closer to them, in class status and life experience, than some of the black kids under the same roof. There is a metaphor there for Eminem's success. He is the first white artist to become an airplay staple on urban radio with predominantly black audiences.

"That is what the film is about, that is what hip-hop is about, and that is why Eminem is who and what he is today," Iovine says. "This movie is about Detroit, but what happened there is happening everywhere."

Detroit, warts and all

Eminem is not Rabbit. "Rabbit shows a much more narrow range of emotions than I do. . . . Jimmy seems to be a more serious, almost depressed and volatile guy," Eminem says in an interview conducted via e-mail. "We don't get to see Jimmy's lighter side in the film."

That may be true, but Eminem's Detroit is the same city where Rabbit runs, and that alone makes it unusual for Hollywood. According to the Michigan film office, "8 Mile" appears to be the first major Hollywood film shot entirely in Detroit. "And it captures the whole intensity of it, the real

Detroit, the burned-out Detroit, out in the bitter cold," says Xzibit, the Detroit-born rapper who plays one of Eminem's rhyming rivals. "It ain't pretty, but it's real."

The realities of Detroit were apparent in the making of a scene that has Rabbit and friends engaging in vigilante redevelopment. In the scene, word is out that the city won't raze an abandoned house that has been the site of a child rape, so Rabbit and his buddies decide to torch it themselves. Upstairs, dousing drawers with gas, Rabbit sees an old photograph of the long-gone residents, a smiling father, mother and their kids, all in their Sunday best. He stares with longing at the image as flames surge behind him.

Hanson added the scene to the script when a local resident shared the real-life account of a neighborhood arson with the same grim motivation. City officials at first refused a permit for the filmed arson—their worry was that destroying an eyesore in a movie might hurt the image of the city as opposed to, say, leaving the building standing. "It is," Hanson says, "pretty crazy if you think about it."

There was another lesson in the making of the scene: The film's art department, heeding Hanson's standing orders of authenticity, scoured Detroit flea markets and thrift stores to find a photo of a Detroit nuclear family, from the 1970s. They could not find a single one. The photograph in the movie was staged; it's a fake family in vintage clothes.

Hanson says he shares the anecdote only to outline the challenges facing young people in Detroit and lack of "traditional signposts for many of them, things such as church and family." He left the city, though, inspired by the people he met and with a deep affection for them. "8 Mile," he says, "is a valentine to the people there."

There are plenty of return valentines for Eminem on both sides of 8 Mile Road these days and he still lives in the city. Crowds often mobbed him during the filming. That's a far cry from the outsider Marshall Mathers. "8 Mile" hopes to take filmgoers on that same journey of understanding, but Iovine reminds again that Rabbit and Eminem are not the same person. The main difference? The music executive answers immediately: "Thirty million albums, worldwide."

GEOFF BOUCHER

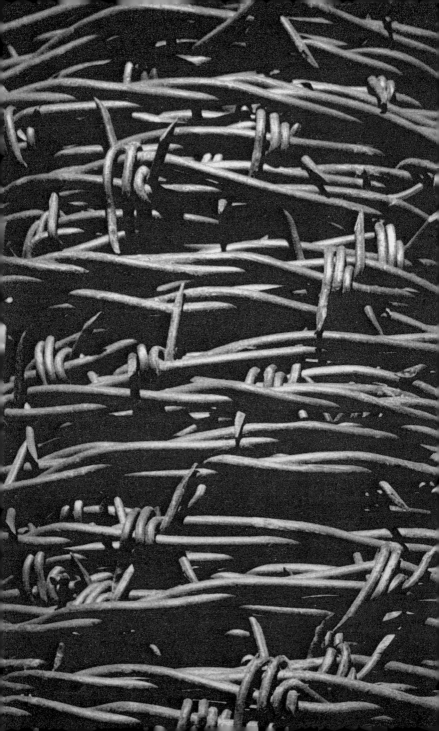

WHITE HOT:

From Rap to Riches

by Elvis Mitchell

from the *New York Times*,
November 8, 2002

the mission of "8 Mile" is essentially to garner sympathy for a white rapper involved in an old-school shootout—a rap contest. This may be the final frontier for pop, more unbelievable than the prospect of launching a member of 'N Sync into orbit. The film's star, Eminem, doesn't appear to have a great deal of range, but he can play himself. Even though the protagonist is named Jimmy Smith, the thoughtful "8 Mile" is a raw version of the rapper's own story.

This is basically an 80's go-for-it movie (the picture feels like some odd combination of "Flashdance" and "Purple Rain"), and the director, Curtis Hanson, working with a screenplay by Scott Silver, has done a fine job of giving it a soul, though it's a gloomy, peeling-paint one. The movie has the echoey, haunted heart of Johnny Cash's cover of Nine Inch Nails' "Hurt": maybe the project doesn't make sense in the abstract, but once you submit to it, it works.

One of a handful of films made in Detroit, "8 Mile" doesn't feature the Motown renaissance that Mayor Coleman A. Young dreamed of in the 1970's. Instead it's the beaten-down city: 8 Mile refers to the line of demarcation between Detroit and suburban, mostly white Oakland County. (The joke is that Oakland County is home to both the megastar white rapper Eminem and the parents who are most afraid of his influence on their kids.)

Mr. Hanson's last two pictures, "L.A. Confidential" and "Wonder Boys," were about the trouble that words can cause. And Jimmy Smith, who is called Rabbit and is determined to be a rapper, spends a great deal of time in hot water because of his mouth. When "8 Mile" begins, Rabbit has moved back into the trailer park home where his mother (Kim Basinger) and little sister Lily (Chloe Greenfield) live, to find that one of his high school friends is now involved with his mom. Rabbit has just broken up with his girlfriend and belongs nowhere. "8 Mile" could be set in a Johnny Cash song, since Rabbit unabashedly refers to himself as white trash.

Rabbit doesn't even fit in at the rap contests in the Detroit club run by his black pal, the dreadlocked entrepreneur Future (Mekhi Phifer). The gray, rust-belt industrial tones captured by the cinematographer Rodrigo Prieto ("Amores Perros") add ominousness to the restroom where Rabbit is sweating as he anxiously waits to take his turn onstage. It's Mr. Hanson's way of cooking up tension. We're always waiting for something to happen, and it occurs at the strangest times and in the strangest juxtapositions, for example, a fight at a radio station. The struggle plays out silently in the background, while the foreground action—an interview in a soundproofed studio—goes on undisturbed.

And it is backstage at the Detroit club, before Rabbit goes out to confront the crowd and compete, that we become aware of his odd remoteness. This is partly because Eminem gives little as an actor. In some ways he's very similar to another white pop-star-turned-actor, Mark Wahlberg. Both have soft, sandpapery voices and a stern politeness when they speak. They're going to make each word count, right down to never dropping a G from the end of an -ing.

Eminem, though, has a relentless, unblinking stare. (It's the expression seen on gifted kids in horror movies.) In contrast to the intensity of his gaze, Eminem's facial muscles are often slack. He has lost weight for his first starring role, and the cleft in his chin has deepened, becoming another shadowy place where he seems to be hiding things. He holds back, waiting, a little nervous. It's only when he gets angry that he comes to life and his voice takes on a shank's edge, dull and rusty.

Rabbit's main competitors—Papa Doc (Anthony Mackie) and his Leaders of the Free World squad—often dismiss him as "Elvis," a white boy appropriating black culture. But when Rabbit starts hollering or rapping, he does indeed give off the explosion of vitality that Presley had while singing in his very early movies. (Here, he becomes the real Slim Shady.)

And like Presley in most of his films, Eminem is given an actressy flirt of a love interest. Her name is Alex, played by the smudge-eyed Brittany Murphy, who can't even walk into a room without sizing up the camera. Exuding a baby-girl narcissism, Alex—who wants to become a model and get out of Detroit—looks at Rabbit as just another opportunity. Taryn Manning, in a much smaller role as Rabbit's ex-girlfriend, is far more believable and makes a bigger impact.

Rabbit keeps his rocket-from-the-crypt ambition focused, doing day work for little money at an auto stamping plant. His real life begins at night when he goes out to compete in hip-hop contests. But he is so unnerved by appearing onstage that,

ELVIS MITCHELL

for most of the picture, Future's faith in the white rapper's skills seems misplaced. Only Future and the millions of record buyers in the moviegoing audience have any idea of Rabbit's abilities. The film is like a rap version of "The Incredible Hulk," and when Rabbit triumphantly rocks the joint at the end, he's flushed, every vein in his body distended—the underdog giving vent to his rage and winning the crowd over. The movie exploits Eminem's slight physical presence, saving the pop-star magnetism for the climax.

"8 Mile," which opens nationwide today, is full of Detroit in-jokes, like Rabbit's referring to himself as "810," one of Oakland County's area codes. And there's a grand-slam joke using the song "Sweet Home Alabama," an omnipresent Motor City radio favorite that has extra resonance in Detroit, a place that refuses to give up its rock 'n' roll roots. It's too bad the movie can't acknowledge that although Detroit was late to rap, it was the birthplace of everything from Motown to the MC5 to Kid Rock. (Kid Rock can also be found on the soundtrack, alongside rap stars like Eric B. and Rakim.) In musical terms, Detroit is like Weimar Berlin, a place where economic and social turbulence create art.

The question is, does "8 Mile" do a convincing job of evoking hip-hop culture? Is the movie real enough for the rap world to take seriously, a question that, applied to himself, has dogged Eminem personally throughout his career. It should be noted that standards are a lot lower for rap movies. After all, Eminem had an almost secret cameo a year ago in "The Wash," a slovenly comedy starring his mentor, Dr. Dre. "8 Mile" is neither as real nor as harrowing as the recent crime film "Paid in Full," which may be the "Mean Streets" of rap. The spirit of rap suffuses "Paid" just as "Streets" encapsulated the intensity of pop.

And what Mr. Hanson has done with "8 Mile" is make a pop movie instead of a movie about pop. There's nothing disreputable about this. The movie is a success on its own terms because the director doesn't condescend to pop music. (As evidenced by the way he used music in "L.A. Confidential," he respects its powers.)

Mr. Hanson keeps the picture alive with the interplay between Rabbit and his crew, which gives it a verbal slapstick flow. The director is great with guys letting down their guard when women aren't around, rapping an impromptu "Pimpin' Ain't Easy" and breaking into brawling locker-room chatter. A winning touch is giving Rabbit's sweet, hapless friend Bob (Evan Jones) the big-money nickname Cheddar.

But the revelation is Mekhi Phifer, who shows a witty cool as Future. Between "8 Mile" and "Paid in Full," he's given his career a revivifying jolt, playing these big-brother roles with an impassioned trust. By not straining to show he's up to the demands of a major picture, he succeeds.

It's too bad "8 Mile" isn't totally as generous as Future—whose real name in the movie is David Porter, which could well be a tribute to Isaac Hayes's songwriting partner. (The movie is full of flavorful pop allusions, including a scene that shows Douglas Sirk's race melodrama "Imitation of Life" playing on a television set. Like Sirk, Mr. Hanson makes movies about coming to grips with one's true identity.)

"8 Mile" could do without an unnecessary class swipe. In a final throwdown, Rabbit clowns a competitor by revealing that the guy went to suburban Detroit Cranbrook, one of the finest private schools in the country. The death of Jam Master Jay, the turntablist of Run-DMC, whose members all hailed from middle-class backgrounds in Queens, reminds us that what's important is the talent you bring to the stage.

On the other hand, the film embraces the absurdity of a white rapper who takes down a brother in a club full of black people—perhaps more black people than own Eminem records. But this fantasy does acknowledge that rap has conquered the world of the young. It's the primary way kids of all races communicate. It's inadvertently hilarious that Eminem scores in this way; with his long, noble nose and porcelain skin, he could be one of the Mies van der Rohe structures on the Cranbrook campus.

MR. AMBASSADOR

by Frank Rich

from the *New York Times*,
November 3, 2002

flashback: It is the year 2000, and Public Cultural Enemy No. 1 is a rapper named Eminem (aka Marshall Mathers III), who has ascended from America's closest approximation of hell (aka his hometown, Detroit). His abundant use of the words "bitch" and "faggot" has aroused the full spectrum of P.C. police, left and right. The violence in his songs is echoed by headlines of his own arrest on gun charges in two consecutive public brawls. And since he is white, he can't be ghettoized: his music is saturating the suburbs at a faster clip than that of black hip-hop artists. Congress, inflamed by Columbine and looking for scapegoats, rounds up the usual suspects for hearings.

But now it is two years later, and on a muggy late summer evening, Eminem is performing before his fans in the Detroit suburbs, the last stop of his 2002 Anger Management Tour. A high point of the show is a song in which he exults in his role as universally despised spokesman for alienated Middle American youth. "White America! I could be one of your kids!" goes its hectoring refrain, insistently gaining in malevolence as if a furious mob were gearing up for a rampage. At its climax he vows to urinate on the White House lawn and hurls expletives at Lynne Cheney and Tipper Gore. But the roaring throng of 16,000 at the Palace of Auburn Hills is not angry. There is barely a whiff of pot in the air, let alone violence. It's a happy crowd, mixed in race and sex, that might just as well have congregated to cheer the Pistons, who also play at the Palace, or at a megachurch or a mall. Even some boomers are on hand (me among them), as well as a few smiling pre-PG-13 kids perched on their dads' shoulders. "It's kind of strange," Eminem would tell me when I asked if he was noticing any difference in his audience of late. "It used to range from 10 years old to 25. Now it seems to be from 5 years old to 55."

Could it be that in just two years the scourge of bourgeois values is now entering the American mainstream? We may find out next weekend, when the country is blanketed with Eminem's debut as a movie star in "8 Mile," a film loosely based on his life. Unlike, say, Prince's "Purple Rain," which always put the musical needs of its star's fan base first, this is a big-studio effort to tap into the national jugular, and it's produced by Brian Grazer, of last year's glossily heart-tugging Oscar champ, "A Beautiful Mind." Grazer is betting that his movie will confirm that Eminem, far from being a public peril, has now "crossed over to the larger demographic."

Should Eminem make that leap, he will hardly be the first pop rebel to do so. When you are the No. 1 act in music, no matter how provocative your songs or how ugly your rap sheet, the culture industry has a vested interest not merely in protecting the franchise but also in expanding it. Moral scolds can condemn each new rock phenomenon as loudly as they like—as they have been doing since the 1950's—but the music is just too contagious and the money too dizzying for anyone in authority to counter the power of a roaring market. Thus has Mick Jagger, the antichrist of Altamont, become both a knight and an establishment corporate franchise, celebrated as a C.E.O. on the cover of Fortune. Ozzy Osbourne is a lovable TV star. Yesterday's "Revolution" can always be tomorrow's Nike commercial.

If there's a particular template for Eminem's career at this early point, it's that of the young Elvis (a comparison that Eminem hates). Both men took a musical form invented by African-Americans and gave it a popular white face. But Eminem has advantages Elvis did not. He writes his own idiosyncratic material rather than singing anyone else's songs. His mentor isn't a white Machiavelli like Colonel Parker, but the legendary hip-hop producer Dr. Dre, whose endorsement gave him instant credibility with black and white audiences alike and shielded him from accusations of cultural theft. ("I am the worst thing since Elvis Presley, to do black music so selfishly and use it to get myself wealthy" goes one of the many Eminem lyrics in which he pre-empts any such criticism.)

That Eminem is also showing Elvis-esque potential to bust out of the youth market is not entirely a surprise. Any listener with open ears and some affinity for the musical vocabulary of hip-hop can easily become hooked on his music. Violence is merely one of the many notes he sounds in a range that stretches from schoolyard slapstick to pathos, and the mayhem is so calculatedly over the top that it seems no more or less offensive than typical multiplex Grand Guignol. In his most ambitious songs, his voice as a writer reaches well beyond idle provocation anyway. He comes at you with a torrent of language that sucks up and spits out the detritus of pop culture (from comic books to Versace) while marrying it to the rage, hurt and, occasionally, love that are at the core of his favorite subject, his own life. Somehow, just when you think he is going to spin out of control, all the rhymes land on their (and the music's) feet, leaving the listener at the end of the precisely observed story he has to tell: the disturbing epistolary chronicle of a deranged fan, the domestic battlefields of both his childhood and his own divorce and, most recently (and sometimes petulantly), the price of fame. In a country in which broken homes, absentee parents and latchkey kids are endemic to every social class, he can touch some of the hottest emotional buttons. He can be puerile too, but what else is new in pop music?

Yet we all know what happened when Elvis, the swivel-hipped menace to American youth, started to broaden his base to the entire country. "The Ed Sullivan Show" may be gone now, but could Eminen find himself yukking it up on Jay Leno's couch? Is there a "Blue Hawaii" in his future? Could he someday end up performing his insult riffs in Vegas, complete with platinum tux to match his famous dyed hair—the hip-hop Don Rickles?

Certainly some sort of transition is under way for Eminem, who turned 30 last month. Though in "White America" he brags about being "in trouble with the government," neither the song nor the video has aroused any new protests from Washington. "It's something that we've blatantly noticed," said Mathers, who is known by his associates as either Marshall or Em, when asked about this unexpected truce. We were meeting on the afternoon of the MTV Video Music Awards, in a Midtown hotel under semi-siege by those under-employed fans who always manage to find out where their icons are holed up. I was there as a sort-of fan myself: I've been fascinated by him ever since I first heard his songs at the inception of his notoriety.

Brian Grazer had told me that when they met, Mathers initially threw him off guard by sitting in glowering silence for minutes on end. The Mathers I met was neither sullen nor wired but straightforward, earnest almost to a fault (his lyrics are fizzier than his conversation), always in direct eye contact and glad to answer any question without hesitation (or any handlers in the room to steer him). He did not seem particularly driven to promote his movie and did not offer a single canned anecdote of the type stars tend to recycle in repeated interviews. Even his regulation hip-hop outfit—Phat Farm sweat pants, T-shirt, bandanna, baseball cap, the inevitable accessories of tattoos and heavy bracelets—looked more lived in than showy.

I asked him to square the present Mathers with the shady Eminem who barely escaped jail (he got three years' probation) for his gun-toting misbehavior of two years ago. "Fame hit me like a expletive ton of bricks," he said. "I was just being pulled in every direction, doing everything under the sun, two shows a day, touring constantly, nonstop radio interviews, and I just got caught up in the drinking and the drugs and fighting and just wilding out and doing dumb things I shouldn't have been doing. But I came out of them and I conquered it. Something really bad could have happened to me. I could be in jail. I could have been shot. I could have been killed. And I'm proud of myself now for not only my accomplishments but for pulling through all that—my criminal cases, my divorce. If I was still on drugs and still living the life that I lived three years ago, I would be a expletive failure." Mathers looks like someone on a gym regimen. His current drug of choice seems to be work, including producing songs by other hip-hop artists for his own new label, Shady Records.

When he occasionally gets into trouble now, it's of a traditional show-business strain—the star boorishness that is our era's version of Frank Sinatra's crude public scuffles. On camera at the MTV awards a few hours after I spoke with him, Mathers insulted the techno-rocker Moby and picked a fight with, of all ridiculous targets, a puppet enacting a comic routine, Robert Smigel's Triumph the Insult Comic Dog. But if the congenitally wary Mathers is still quick to lash back at any person or toy he feels may be dissing him, the blows are all verbal, and most reports of his behavior are glowing. This summer People magazine celebrated him as an ideal joint-custody father to his daughter, Hailie, 6, who is the one angelic female subject (and occasional vocal participant) in his canon, and as a model neighbor who attends community meetings no less, in his gated community in the northern Detroit suburbs.

"My daughter is growing up, and I'm trying to set an example for her," Mathers said, warming to the only subject besides hip-hop that lightens him up. "She has a fairly normal life. I love her so much. And she's a character, man. She's like me to the 10th power, she's got such a personality. She runs around the house and she makes up little sayings and little phrases."

"8 Mile," which not only has a blue-chip producer in Grazer but an A-list director in Curtis Hanson (of "L.A. Confidential" and "Wonder Boys"), hardly presents Eminem as a family man, but it does burnish his image. The movie describes a week in the Detroit 1995 life of Jimmy Smith Jr.— a fictional character who, despite protestations from the star and everyone else associated with the film, is closer in biographical outline to Marshall Mathers III than not. Jimmy is a white-trash high-school dropout trapped in menial labor and living in desolate trailer-park circumstances around Eight Mile Road. "It's the borderline of what separates suburb from city," Mathers explains. "It's the color line. I grew up on both sides of it and saw everything. I had the friends who had racist redneck fathers and stepfathers. I had black friends. It's just American culture."

Like Mathers, Jimmy was abandoned at birth by his father. To his chagrin, he still lives with his mother (played by Kim Basinger), an irresponsible alcoholic who vaguely resembles the real-life mother depicted in Eminem songs and videos (and who sued him twice for defamation, netting only $1,600). Though Jimmy has a love interest (Brittany Murphy), the real love of his life is a much younger kid sister who in age and adorability could be a stand in for the real-life Hailie. Jimmy's only other burning passion is his music. Like his black pals, he dreams of somehow recording a demo, getting a deal, hooking up with a star producer like Dr. Dre and going platinum. By the movie's end, you sense he's on his way—a white underdog likely to make good.

Grazer concedes that one reason he fictionalized his protagonist was the harsh criticism he received for taking liberties with the biography of John Nash, the subject of "A Beautiful Mind." Of course, fiction provides other benefits as well. If "A Beautiful Mind" was criticized for eliminating some homosexual incidents in John Nash's life, "8 Mile" goes out of its way to neutralize Eminem's reputation, deserved or not, for homophobia.

At this point not all that much more repair work may be needed. Gay organizations have lowered their voices since the 2001 Grammys, at which Elton John came out of the closet as an Eminem fan and performed a duet with him on camera. Nonetheless, it's a telling digression in "8 Mile" when its hero rushes to the rescue of a fellow metal-plant worker who has been mocked for being gay. Jimmy's intervention takes the form of a hilarious rap pointedly denigrating the bigoted bully, rather than the ridiculed gay man, as a "faggot." The sequence is shrewdly designed to buttress Mathers's argument that when "faggot" appears in his songs it is either: a) spoken in the voice of Eminem's nasty fictional hip-hop alter ego, Slim Shady, who does not literally represent the views of his creator; or b) being used, as it is by many kids, as an all-purpose insult "not meant to be literal." Mathers says now that he has never been a homophobe: "It's really none of my business. I don't give a expletive what your sexual preferences are. As long as you're cool with me, I'm cool with you."

But the most fascinating image enhancement in "8 Mile" is the ease with which it fits a character as rough and ostensibly subversive as Eminem into a smooth and reassuring show-business fable as old as "The Jazz Singer." The movie's plot hinges on Jimmy's ability to overcome his paralyzing shyness and compete in freestyle rapping battles—open-mike contests in which rival aspiring hip-hop artists try to top one another with artfully rhymed invective, the winner determined by audience cheers. As Jimmy at first prepares for and ultimately triumphs in his battles, he could be John Travolta's Tony Manero trying to escape outer-borough drudgery by dancing his way to the top in the disco-era "Saturday Night Fever" or Diana Ross escaping the ghetto in "Mahogany" or Sissy Spacek's Loretta Lynn emerging from poverty in "Coal Miner's Daughter" or even Barbra Streisand's Fanny Brice rising from her ethnic urban ghetto to show-biz triumph in "Funny Girl."

This is not unintentional. When talking about cinematic archetypes for "8 Mile," Paul Rosenberg, the burly, low-key 31-year-old lawyer who manages Mathers, says that the movie hopes to tap "the same sort of cultural phenomenon as 'Saturday Night Fever.'" Curtis Hanson, who at 57 is on the outer edge of the new Eminem demographic, prepared his crew for "8 Mile" by screening, among other films, "Hoop Dreams," the 1994 documentary about two teenage athletes from inner-city Chicago aspiring to break into basketball superstardom. He says that he hopes that the Eminem/Jimmy story could be inspirational in a similar way. "Churches, schools, family are supposed to give structure to kids," he says, "but now they're all part of a dysfunctional culture. No one's helping kids figure out where they're going—not just in the inner cities but in the suburbs. Hip-hop comes out of that. It is a voice for people who don't have another voice."

Unlike Elvis, who usually parachuted into mechanical Hollywood vehicles that were built around his songs, Mathers and Rosenberg helped develop "8 Mile." The movie banks on the star's persona and backstory rather than on his greatest hits, and while he is in every scene, he never does a full-dress number like those in his videos. The star and what he calls his "team" were aware of the possible pitfalls. "It could have ended up like 'Woe is me, poor little Marshall went through so much,'" Mathers says.

"Marshall's biggest fear—mine as well—was that it would look phony," Brian Grazer says. "I make these bigger mainstream movies, and if all of a sudden I decide to make a street movie and make it corny, I look like a clown." Hanson insisted that "8 Mile" be shot in the festering precincts of Detroit—in lieu of blander, cheaper Canada—and he also put Mathers through six weeks of rehearsals, in essence an acting class, before starting to shoot. (A more typical rehearsal period, Grazer says, is two days to two weeks.)

The star did not pretend to enjoy the experience, which he likened to boot camp: "It was anywhere between 13 and 16 hours a day, six days a week. It literally gave me enough time to go to sleep, get up and come back and do the movie." But however ambivalent he may be about the medium, he obsesses over the quality of the result as much as he does over his music. I asked, Are you happy with "8 Mile"? "I'm getting happier every time I see a new cut of it," he allowed.

He clearly had bothered Hanson about every detail. "I'm like, yo, watch my facial expression here, it's not the greatest in the world," he said in describing his post-production interplay with the director. "And he found other takes. I always thought the story was good, but I want everything to be perfect. Every time I felt like I wasn't believable I took notes, and I brought them to Curtis." Now that it's over, he is in no mood even to watch movies: "It's because I'm looking for continuity and looking for mistakes. The guy's shirt's a little wrinkled, and you cut back and it's the same scene and his shirt's not wrinkled. You drive yourself crazy with it."

For his part, Hanson says he didn't take on the assignment until he was satisfied Mathers was serious. "Was he making this movie simply because he could? I didn't know if he would apply his attention to this or be a dilettante about it," he says. "And he was assessing me, too; he asked a lot of questions about the mechanics. We had ups and downs, but he gave me everything a director could want. He gave me a commitment and a kind of respect." Mathers also developed a respect for those who take acting as seriously as he takes his music. "Kim Basinger normally doesn't rehearse," Hanson says, "and in her first scene, when she came out full-bore, Marshall was knocked back on his heels. He said, 'I kind of like this acting thing.'"

Mathers delivered an intense screen presence—far more effective than that of his touring show, where his loose-limbed performance style and diminutive stature require a busy supporting cast and scads of visual effects to fill the stage. But Mathers isn't looking for a movie career and mainly hopes the film will explain his missionary zeal for hip-hop to the uninitiated. Music was the refuge, he feels, from a childhood defined by domestic chaos and ostracization by his peers. "I wanted to make a movie that every kid who went through anything similar to this can relate to," he says. "This was my whole life. If I lost a battle at the hip-hop shop when I was coming up, it literally tore me apart inside."

If the older audience that thinks rap is merely vulgar noise shows up for "8 Mile"—a big if—it will find that the movie makes a credible case as well for hip-hop as a positive social good. After all, the rap battles that form the crux of the film,

reminiscent of boxing matches and given full "Raging Bull" treatment by Hanson, make the legitimate point that it is a rapper's imagination that counts most in hip-hop success. When Jimmy squares off with his rival in a battle, its substance has more in common with a no-holds-barred debating competition than an urban brawl; it is screen violence in which language substitutes for fists. "At the end of the day hip-hop is about brainpower," says Mathers. "It's brain versus brain. It's about who can outsmart who." What better role model could any parent ask for?

Whatever the fate of "8 Mile," it is certain that the culture wars about hip-hop in general and Eminem in particular are nearly kaput. "Bin Laden stopped that," says Jimmy Iovine of Interscope Records, Eminem's label. "9/11 showed that Joe Lieberman should have been managing the F.B.I. and the C.I.A. instead of trying to manage my company."

But that's not the whole story. Hip-hop has become so big that it is now by definition the cultural norm, not the rebellious exception to it. "People are accepting Eminem because he's a superstar," Grazer says. "They don't even question things from his past—or have forgotten them." Iovine notes that "at first hip-hop freaked out Hollywood because it wasn't rock 'n' roll." Some executives agreed with the politicians' condemnations. But no one argues any longer with its success. Music this popular has the power to move all kinds of markets. Product placement in hip-hop songs can be a bonanza, as witness "Pass the Courvoisier Part II," by Busta Rhymes, which increased the brandy's sale by 4.5 percent in the first quarter of this year. Sean John Combs, aka Puff Daddy and P. Diddy, emerged from acquittal in his trial in a 1999 Manhattan nightclub shooting incident to become a men's wear fashion arbiter. This fall's surprise feel-good hit, drawing white moviegoers as well as black, was the hip-hop-flecked "Barbershop," starring Ice Cube.

Mathers prides himself on sticking to his own artistic impulses, no matter how the scene changes around him. Asked why his audience is broadening, he cites his own growth. "In my heart I wanted to solidify myself as an artist and show that as I grow as a person and make mistakes and learn from them I'm going to grow artistically," he says. "And maybe that's what's attracting this older audience.

"I'm always going to be me no matter what," he adds. "There's always going to be a part of me that's going to be as raw as when I first came out. There's always going to be that part that I can revert to if I want to go back and be that battle M.C. and say those funny punch lines and stuff to make people laugh or make people angry. But as I grow as a person and as I get older I've got to mature. If you think that the only way I can make a record is by cussing, then I'll make a different record to outsmart you and prove you wrong. But every song that I make has to be better than the last one that I just made. Otherwise it gets scrapped. Because if you're not doing that, you're stagnant. If I wanted to, I could drop an album of all the songs that didn't make it on my record and sell a million or two or whatever just to get money. I'm not about that."

Iovine, whose career began as an engineer on Bruce Springsteen's "Born to Run," says he thinks Mathers has "the chops to make the transition" to a long-term artistic career. "I've been fortunate to be at the turning points of Lennon, Springsteen, Bono," he says. "I've watched them all go through massive changes of direction. When you have an artist this great, you have to move forward. You'll lose people here and there, but those there in the beginning will always be there for him."

In my conversation with Mathers, he didn't seem remotely caught up in whether he remained Public Enemy No. 1 or in his own commercial fate—or in that of "8 Mile." He was instead preoccupied in his finicky, worry-wart way with the job at hand, much like his alter ego in the movie, who is often found meticulously perfecting the lyrics he prints in a tiny hand on scrap paper with a ballpoint pen. He had been up until 5 a.m. the night before tweaking the music on the movie's soundtrack, which had followed rehearsals for the MTV show. He disdained the idea of ever leaving Detroit to "get a $10 million home in New York or Hollywood and just be extravagant." He says he watches his money closely and is always thinking about his daughter's financial future. His own future? "Eventually I want to branch off into being a producer and be able to one day sit back like Dre and kind of be behind the scenes and not always have to be the front man."

For now, though, he seems more in demand as a star than ever. As "8 Mile" was awaiting its premiere, every establishment TV show from "Today" to "60 Minutes" was approaching Marshall Mathers. Lynne Cheney and Congressional scolds notwithstanding, even the United States government has joined the Eminem bandwagon: this summer it started broadcasting his songs in the Middle East as part of its propaganda campaign to enhance America's image to young radio listeners in the Arab world.

NOISE

WHITE MAN'S BURDEN

Eminem's Movie Debut in *8 Mile*

by Roy Grundmann

from *Cineaste*, Spring 2003

virtually unknown twenty-five years ago, rap music today is a multimillion dollar business and a global cultural force. Originally appearing in the mid-Seventies in New York's South Bronx as part of hip hop, a larger spectrum of newly emerging artistic forms that include graffiti and breakdancing, rap became the musical expression of choice for impoverished and disenfranchised inner-city blacks. Covered by the protective cloak of ghetto subculture, rap went largely unnoticed until the eve of the Eighties, when the Sugar Hill Gang's "Rapper's Delight" became rap's first smash hit. By the early Nineties, rap had become fully commercialized, but it had also evolved into an impressive diversity of styles with acts ranging from the aggressively masculine L.A.

gangsta rap of Ice-T to what critics have labeled rap's Native Tongues wing—with Queen Latifah and Brand Nubian, among others, emphasizing Afrocentricity and anti-sexism.

Like blues, jazz, soul, and early rock 'n' roll, rap is a musical form whose cross-over popularity is proof yet again that white America has always been deeply fascinated by black culture. Yet, just like blues, jazz and soul (though less than rock 'n' roll), rap has also attracted a certain amount of white talent, and, within the past three years, it has produced its first white superstar. Eminem's most recent musical effort, *The Eminem Show*, was the number one album of 2002, and his previous albums have likewise outsold the biggest rap and nonrap acts in the U.S. and abroad. Eminem's popularity is much more easily acknowledged than explained because, like the appeal of the biggest, most famous and most enduring talents in show business, it is complex and has several roots. More particularly, it reflects a combination of factors typical for successful rap performers: an undeniable lyrical talent (expressed through but also beyond notorious off-color rants); a well-developed apocalyptic sensibility (particularly with regard to picturing social anarchy), a richly faceted public persona (Eminem is never just Eminem—he inhabits a coterie of personas, most prominently the sleazy and diabolical 'Slim Shady,' through whom he speaks and behind whom he hides against charges of obscenity); and a marketing juggernaut that knows how to combine all these factors and propel him to fame.

The debate about the virtues and drawbacks of Eminem's art is just as complicated as the art itself. On one hand, he has become the *enfant terrible* for civil-rights groups and lobbyists who condemn violence, sexual obscenity, and verbal discrimination in all commercial art and call for the entertainment industry's (self)regulation (the nature and frequency of the charges make one wonder if any of these groups and individuals would have given Eminem half as much attention had he been black). On the other hand, proliferating attacks have triggered a groundswell of support in the past three years. At one point or another, everyone seemed to be taking a stand, from Lynne Cheney to Madonna, from Bill Clinton to Elton John. Some defenses seem more valid than others. Consider, for example, Eminem's own argument that he is merely playing devil's advocate—perhaps in the tradition of such lowbrow, free-form comedians as Lenny Bruce, or such highbrow verbal wizards as Vladimir Nabokov. This argument, while valid in principle, still smacks of a cop-out. As a form of popular culture, rap has a much wider, more visceral impact on its audience than modernist literature such as *Lolita* or intricate comedy such as that of Bruce.

More insightful is the argument that his verse of vice, when examined closely, have a complexity that tends to get lost in performance. Far from constituting a one-kind-of-rant-fits-all-approach, the lyrics do, in fact, fall into several categories that sometimes splinter into internal, rather self-reflexive dialogs, and that seek to combine, in various shades and intensities, the political with the personal and the obscene with the socially conscious. Like carnivalesque art, Eminem's rap pieces are often satirical attacks against the government, the police, and middle-class hypocrisy. To be sure, these attacks are fleeting asides; their brevity prevents them from becoming systematic critiques of society. They do, however, testify to a certain complexity in his art. In fact, like much of carnivalesque art, Eminem's lyrics are in elaborate dialog with themselves. In his song "Guilty Conscience," for example, he debates whether he should rob a liquor store, have sex with a drugged-out fifteen year old (girl), and slit his cheating wife's throat.

No matter how graphic these debates, their outcome remains unresolved; they picture the horror of unsupervised, adolescent ghetto life with the same visceral realism as Larry Clark's indie shocker, *Kids* (a movie Eminem refers to in one of his songs). There is a certain legitimacy to the argument that, rather than ignoring or suppressing violent teen fantasies (the way many parents and schools do), these lyrics directly address them. While some claim that showing violence breeds more violence, Eminem supporters have a point in claiming that, curiously, it is Eminem and Marilyn Manson, not urban-crime dramas such as *Training Day* or military spectacles such as *Black Hawk Down*, that tend to get blamed for inspiring high-school shootings. Ironically, Eminem himself has acknowledged the potential traps of violent song content. His song "Sam," for example, stages a debate between himself and a fictitious fan who can no longer distinguish between reality and the Eminem songs he tries to emulate.

The carnivalesque character of the Eminem phenomenon is reflected no less in the wildly heterogeneous nature of his fan base. Naturally, it includes many young white middle-class consumers, for they exercise the buying power to make superstars. But if one is to believe fan websites, Eminem's popularity transcends the boundaries of race and ethnicity as easily as it does those of suburb and inner city. In fact, one of his recent albums did quite well in a music popularity poll conducted by *The Village Voice*, whose readership is unlikely to support an artist who is merely a misogynist and a homophobe. Vilified by GLAAD and NOW, but supported by Madonna and performing with Elton John at the Grammy Awards, Eminem has reached the kind of success that is unclassifiable, and matched only by the irrationality of the media circus that surrounds him. He was a centerpiece in MTV's recent Music Video Awards, although he was sandwiched between comedians Jim Carrey, who called his lyrics "socially irresponsible," and a Public Service Announcement read by Matthew Shepard's mother.

However outlandish Eminem's tirades, they only partly account for his appeal. No matter how much his fans may recognize his talent, for example, it is also the skillful show-biz manipulation of his working-class background that goes straight to the cash register. His class roots show in just the right way at the right moment, as does his vaguely exotic street sensibility, which appeals to many suburban teens. His street cred also renders his racial makeup more complex than his lily-white skin suggests. He may not be black, but he has a darkness all his own. Unlike his predecessor, Vanilla Ice, Eminem has understood that black rappers' relation to 'whitey' gives them a very specific integrity. Black rappers may appeal partly, even largely, to the same audience as Eminem, but they do so with an attitude their white counterparts would be wise not to emulate blindly. Thus, Eminem has wisely kept a respectful distance from sensitive areas, while making the various raw deals he's been dealt the subject of his own art— a rough childhood spent in back-and-forth transit between Kansas City and Detroit, followed by an even rougher youth as a trailer-park dweller, a high-school dropout, and a minimum wage laborer—all of which is offset by a Dionysian way with words which, alas, made him an outcast yet again, this time racially.

With Eminem, show business has coughed up a dirty little white boy who has appropriated a black art form and is milking it for its worth. Needless to say, it was just a matter of time before movies appeared on the horizon. But while rap's success is synonymous with its appropriation by Hollywood, a distinction must be drawn between the recording industry and the movie business. In contrast to the big music labels' swift and avaricious consumption of rap during the Eighties, its deployment by the big studios has been considerably more measured, which reflects movie producers' usual approach to all non-white, non-middle class matters. Rap scores may have proven essential to the niche marketing of 'Hood films and some black-themed urban-crime dramas, but a movie meant to function as a detailed visual index of rap's fantasies—which range from the angry to the nihilistic—about the white Establishment and white-controlled Law and Order is a different matter altogether. The film industry's effective banalization and containment of the charismatic Tupac Shakur (one of Eminem's idols) in John Singleton's inane *Poetic Justice* is a good indication of the studios wariness of a star vehicle for a rap performer.

If Eminem's Slim Shady persona holds a certain appeal, then, it is less because producers want to exploit his sleaze in its full beauty for the big screen, and more because they find his rather conventional side appealing. His masochistic abjection makes him a classic underdog ("Ninety-five percent of my life I was lied to"); his white lower-class anger contains just the right ratio of moderately incisive social analysis and highly personal rage; and, finally, the hatred of his mother has propelled Slim Shady into the long line of American protagonists who suffer from 'Momism,' a form of misogyny particularly popular in the Fifties, but one that can still drive a movie plot. Mother has made sure that Slim suffers from a full-fledged virgin/whore complex (in his rap songs, of course, it is his little daughter who is the virgin). But too much attention to the opposite sex has always harmed the American movie hero, and while Slim is more of an antihero, he shares with the classic movie hero a core of rugged individualism and a dogged determination that appeals to a mainstream audience.

Given this kind of star appeal, one might assume that Slim, at one point or another, would have mustered the gumption to pack up and go to Hollywood. Instead, it was Hollywood who sought him out. Movie producer Brian Grazer explained in an interview that he had been planning to make a new variant of the *Saturday Night Fever/Flashdance* formula, transposed into the world of rap—except, of course, that the film was not to depict the "problematic" content of rap songs but rather the everyday life of a 'normal' fan turned rapper. The finished film, 8 *Mile*, loosely reflects not only certain details of Mathers's life but also early stages of Eminem's career. Set in 1995, its drama conveys the struggle of a white rap artist in a black music scene (which reflects the negative reception of Eminem's first album, *Infinite*); its dramatis personae draws on Eminem's decision to get a black mentor (Dr. Dre, who has also become his producer); and its depiction of the protagonist's talent and testiness derives from the fact that 'battling'—rapping with black rappers in a contest—has always been Eminem's second nature.

Directed by Curtis Hanson (*Wonder Boys*, *L.A. Confidential*), Eminem plays Jimmy Smith Jr., affectionately called "Rabbit" by friends and family. He is a white boy living in Detroit's predominantly black inner city area that is demarcated from the affluent white suburbs in the north by 8 Mile Road, the thoroughfare that gives the film its title. Having grown up in a trailer park, Rabbit is 'white trash.' But he has been imbibing black inner-city culture—its mannerisms, codes of conduct, lingo, and, of course, its music. In fact, he has become a master of 'freestyling' (the art of the impromptu rap salvo), and his talent lands him on stage at the Shelter, a joint where every Friday night local performers compete in feverish rap battles. We first encounter Rabbit preparing for his act in the club's dank men's room. His intense stare at his mirror image and his masterful command of rap's body language cannot conceal the fact that he has the jitters, and when he can no longer keep his food down, we know he must have reason to be nervous. Once on stage, disaster promptly unfolds. Stunned by his opponent's put-down and intimidated by the crowd, he freezes, then flees the scene.

The rest of the film consists of a string of fairly banal episodes—Rabbit breaking up with his girl, moving back into his mom's trailer, meeting a new girl, beating up his mom's

ROY GRUNDMANN

cad boyfriend, looking after his kid sister, holding on to his job at an auto plant, hanging with his homeboys (who are 'bad' in a ghetto sort of way but, of course, still really nice guys), getting beaten up by other homeboys (the gang of his nemesis, whose leader turns out to be a ghetto poseur, are truly bad), and so on—all the while, of course, writing his rap rhymes and honing his craft. All this is to show, simply, how Rabbit gradually 'finds himself' and regains the gumption to return to the Shelter and battle for victory, the outcome of which, needless to say, is never in doubt.

A rite-of-passage drama of sorts, 8 Mile is as simplistic as it is contrived. But it has a purpose. Systematically inviting us to conflate Eminem with his fictional character, 8 Mile's *raison d'etre* is to persuade us that the world should hold a rightful place for a white virtuoso of black art. At second glance, this may not be all that horrible. At this point in music history, there doesn't seem to be any danger that whites will eventually take over hip hop the way they took over rock 'n' roll in the late Fifties. While Eminem's latest album topped the charts last year, the black rapper Nelly claimed a number two place in total sales during the same period. Eminem's producer, Dr. Dre, sold six million of his most recent album. In the meantime, Eminem is reportedly helping some black talent in Detroit get record deals.

It's arguable whether 8 Mile represents the 'mainstreaming' of Eminem. His success and his broad-based fan community imply that he is already mainstream, sort of. Hollywood is simply trying to cash in on a phenomenon already in place, just as it pounced on Presley, Sinatra, and the Beatles after they had achieved stardom with their music. On the other hand, if mainstreaming means to garner support for Eminem's work among those who never listen to (much less buy) rap music, then Eminem's desire to stake out his claim is promoted more effectively in the realm of movie mythology. Nevertheless, 8

Mile depicts whites and blacks as part of the same underclass, as victims sharing the same fate rather than enemies constantly at each other's throat. It tries to present a realistic drama of race relations marked by a daily, unspectacular peace, or at least an everyday apathy, rather than by high octane animosity and warfare. While the white virtuoso of black art, however, depends on black approval and is entitled to black communal respect, 8 *Mile* suggests that black friendship or making mixed-race communitarian art is ultimately no alternative to romantic white solitude. Rabbit will always remain a white working-class loner. This would be an interesting point if it were analyzed within the framework of the depressed status and isolation of both races, but the film merely creates the kind of convenient mythological shorthand that relieves audiences from giving this matter any further thought.

Given its agenda, it is no surprise that 8 *Mile* comes off as one big orgy of black hands patting a white back. Rabbit's black friends never really question him: when he growls at them, they sensitively understand; when he calls them losers, they become intrigued and pensive. In turn, they are paragons of loyalty and support. Rabbit's most important friend is Future (Mekhi Phifer). He is the self-effacing linchpin of Rabbit's transformation. A soul mate and fellow artist, Future confronts Rabbit with his own 'white-trash' background and inspires him to embrace his identity on an artistic level. But Future also acts as a mediator between his own people and his white friend, gaining him access to all levels of black culture. When a bouncer blocks Rabbit's entry into the club, it takes only one word from Future to clear the path. Future also happens to be the Emcee of the rap contest at the Shelter, and he uses his position to promote his white buddy and to subtly ingratiate him to the jaded black audience.

Mekhi Phifer's radiance infuses the character with an almost otherworldly glow and goodwill. He is at his most

ROY GRUNDMANN

suave when he and his friends encounter another group on a parking lot that at night doubles as a hip-hop meeting ground for rappers. A master of crowd manipulation and eager to join the party, Future signals peaceful intent and respect of territory, skillfully handling the volatile dynamics of inter- as well as cross-racial encounter. He steps into the other group's circle and introduces his own posse with a rap about the tyranny of boundaries, categories, and norms, and the need to break them: "We even keep a white boy or two," he quips, disarmingly paving the way for Rabbit, who has self-effacingly lingered in the background and who, for a few seconds, gently protests being pulled into the ring. A few seconds later, of course, Rabbit has taken over the show.

Like other scenes in *8 Mile*, the parking-lot scene draws on the early stages in Eminem's career. Those who attended his early gigs or followed *Rolling Stone's* early concert coverage know that Eminem always has himself introduced on stage by black rapper MC Proof and that he took care to surround himself with black friends. While the scenes at the Shelter are meant to show how Rabbit/Eminem wins the respect of a savvy and critical black audience, the parking-lot scene is meant to show how his skills win him the respect of the entire black subculture. From the standpoint of this subculture, however, the parking-lot scene and the film in general are counterproductive, because Eminem's overbearing presence takes from rap more than it gives: it erases rap's history before the film can reference it, overlooking or simply ignoring many of rap's historical and cultural details.

The parking-lot scene in *8 Mile* is vaguely evocative of 'playing the dozens' a traditional African-American street contest in which competitors engage in poetic repartee, often taunting each other with insults about a family's lineage. In fact, the film shows the contemporary street version of this contest, called 'the cypher,' in which a group of rappers take turns freestyling in a tight circle, meant to provide protection and spiritual intimacy. At least one more important piece of the historical puzzle can be found in rap's early history, with its spontaneous street parties during which such legendary DJs as Grandmaster Flash and DJ Kool Herc introduced rappers onto the floor to engage and stimulate the crowd. According to the chroniclers of rap, such as Tricia Rose, some of these rappers engaged in boasting and toasting—two Afro-Caribbean forms of oral storytelling that flaunt the 'bad,' ruthless qualities of the teller in aggressive and violent scenarios (which reportedly made them popular with late-Sixties black militants). This spectacle egged the crowd on and became such a hit that an open mike soon invited audience participation, initiating the spontaneous rap contest on which *8 Mile* in too cavalier of a fashion bases its on- and off-stage battles.

Another example of *8 Mile*'s ethnographic approach to rap culture is the lunch-break scene at the auto plant in which a male worker puts a female coworker down for complaining about her lousy job and pay. The fight instantly evolves into a rap battle, but the male rapper is unusually abrasive, picking harshly not only on the woman but also on an openly gay colleague next to her. Rabbit puts the attacker in his place with his own virtuoso versioning of the putdown. Hanson explained in an interview that he intended the scene to be a mini lecture for viewers about the history of rap (focusing on three stages—social protest, ugly and nasty anger, and smart, witty performance). But the scene undermines its own mission to educate in the way it glosses rap and its combatants. To begin with, Rabbit's counterattack is questionable for more than one reason. His coming to the aid of his female and gay coworkers is a transparent attempt to soften Eminem's well-known image as a misogynist and homophobe. To make matters worse, what was intended as damage control turns into the opposite, as the script flaunts Rabbit's conviction that the only suitable putdown for a homophobe is to one up him by accusing him of being HIV positive. A less obvious but similarly egregious problem with this scene is that what began as a fairly explicit reference to oppressive labor conditions is quickly personalized and turned into a carnival for the audience. Just as the earlier parking-lot scene is abruptly terminated by invoking the bad gangsta 'ex machina' who breaks up the party and randomly picks a fight, the lunch break scene, too, individualizes and, hence, depoliticizes in classic Hollywood manner both race and class relations.

Given Hollywood's tendency to merely gloss local color, Eminem should be commended for insisting that 8 *Mile* be shot entirely on location in Detroit. In one or two instances, actual Detroit locations are recognizable, such as the art deco building turned parking lot which, according to Detroiters who have been polled about their impression of the film, catches the atmosphere and architectural history of the city well. At first glance, one gets the impression that the film attempts to commercially exploit inner-city topography for the kind of minutely detailed and authentic ghetto specifically found in black rap-music videos and early Nineties 'Hood films. The same is true for many rap-music videos, which insist on the recognizability of the ghetto, especially since it often remains the rap performer's home base. Ghetto specificity has led to a phenomenon appreciated by audiences and analyzed by critics: the emergence of veritable cross-country music video dialogs between performers such as Ice Cube (South Central Los Angeles) and Naughty by Nature (East Orange, New Jersey), for whom the home base is a source of pride and an integral part of their persona and image.

More often than not, however, the locations featured in 8 *Mile* remain a mere backdrop. One extended scene of Rabbit's bus ride to work is intended as a 'sightseeing tour' of Detroit. Looking out the window while composing his rap rhymes,

Rabbit sees ramshackle warehouses, boarded-up and dilapidated residences, shuttered stores, and large stretches of urban wasteland go by—images familiar to the neglected inner-city districts of many American cities. Impressionistically photographed by Rodrigo Prieto (*Frida, Amores Perros*) and further estheticized by production designer Philip Messina, who gave the Mexican sequence of Steven Soderbergh's *Traffic* the look of a tobacco commercial, *8 Mile* deftly depicts 'Detroit-ness' while showing surprisingly little of actual Detroit.

Another contradiction in *8 Mile*'s portrayal of Detroit inner-city life is its handling of the 'gun issue.' As a lurid look at the ghetto, the film, on one hand, seems compelled to exploit its fictional setting for the generic spectacle of violence, while, on the other hand, the film's liberal impulse is to show that guns are not synonymous with mundane ghetto existence. Rabbit and his posse are 'good' slum kids—they know better than to fool around with guns. The film's solution to the conflicting demands of entertainment is to give the kids guns that look real but turn out to be paint-ball rifles, which they fire from their barely functional car into store windows and parked police vehicles. The film can thus play it cute (a drive-by shooting turns into a drive-by paint job) and still sustain the vague ambience of vehicular ghetto warfare. Brashness and buffoonery are similarly kept in balance when Rabbit's only white buddy Cheddar Bob (Evan Jones) attempts to break up a fist fight by pulling out a real gun but, hapless and crazed, literally shoots himself in the foot. When the film eventually ups the ante in a third gun scene, it is, predictably, the black guy, Papa Doc, who gets to wield the piece, even if he stops short of pulling the trigger on Rabbit. Papa Doc's association with the threat of murder may be invidious, but it is ultimately only one example among many of *8 Mile*'s brand of ghetto ethnography.

8 Mile is somewhat more successful in portraying Rabbit's 'trailer-trash' existence. While no more specifically related to

Detroit than the film's other generalized settings, the cluttered old trailer and its bleak surroundings do come across as an authentic source for Rabbit's anger. The production design and hand-held interior cinematography here are greatly aided by Kim Basinger's performance as Stephanie, Rabbit's mother. Perhaps because her acting resume is studded with dumb-blonde and sex-bomb roles, critics still have a hard time discussing her as a serious actress (oops, actor). Her Southern accent, for example, is credible—one of the film's few inspired references to Detroit demographics, suggesting the mass migration of southerners to the North during the postwar economic boom.

Increasingly evoking such performers as Gloria Grahame these days, Basinger rises to the arduous task of portraying Rabbit's smash-up mom. Hers is an important role not only because she is the epicenter of the Smith family's domestic dysfunction, but also because the film's polemical conflation of Rabbit with the real-life rapper who plays him are bound to trigger associations with Mama Mathers, the bane of Marshall's existence. Basinger makes the best of what the role has to offer, crafting the portrait of a weak and beaten woman who, tragically yet typically, clings to her physically and emotionally abusive boyfriend (Michael Shannon). She nervily slams through an increasingly cliché-ridden script which demands, for example, that Stephanie leave out no opportunity to appear to Rabbit a 'bad,' irresponsible mother, but which ends in a conciliatory pancake orgy after she wins a bundle at bingo.

Before it turns into pure cornball, 8 Mile's trailer-park realism fulfills two important functions: first, it conveys much of the source of Rabbit's anger, as it outlines the downward spiral of parental neglect, emotional exploitation, and bitter recrimination; second, it provides the rhetorically crucial backdrop to his transformation from 'white trash' into 'proud

white trash.' Not unlike Rocky Balboa, Rabbit has to endure a
series of humiliations. These supposedly make him stronger,
because they are accompanied by experiences of abjection
which paradoxically bring the hero 'back in touch with himself.' (Masochism, as long as it's redemptive, is actually central
to patriarchal culture.) But Rabbit's masochism, unlike
Rocky's, is of a more self-righteous kind, and the sadism into
which it tilts over is also politically more volatile.

When Rabbit finally meets Papa Doc eye to eye on the
stage of the Shelter, his strategy is a direct result of his transformation: before directing his aggression towards his opponent, he first directs it against himself, rattling off a litany of
self-deprecating admissions that amount to something like, 'I
may be white trash, but I'm still standing in front of you!'
Having thus preempted any counterattack, he then debunks
Papa Doc as an upper-middle-class windbag who went to a
prestigious private school, an offensive move which instantly
wins him the sympathies of the black under-dog-loving crowd.
The film thus erects his protagonist's white working-class
pride at the expense of Papa Doc's middle-class status, which,
as we are told, is cause for scandal. The 'reverse racism' that
Rabbit has purportedly been experiencing throughout the
entire movie is thus transformed into a reverse classism that is
turned against Papa Doc. In fact, with the exception of
Stephanie's boyfriend, Greg, the film's only two really negative characters, Papa Doc and Wink (Eugene Byrd), the
shifty and deceptive 'promoter,' are both black and middle
class or, at least, upwardly mobile.

Having defeated Papa Doc, Rabbit has fully staked his
claim before a black audience, and even the bouncer who
earlier blocked his entry signals approval. The film has com-
pleted its legitimation narrative, albeit with a twist that directly reflects Eminem's image as a dirty white boy. In contrast
to Vanilla Ice, who faced charges from the hip-hop commu-

nity of trying to be a 'wigger' (a 'white nigger,' an updated version of Norman Mailer's 'White Negro'), Eminem long ago learned to embrace his whiteness—flaunting it with pride and self-consciously manipulating and resignifying its implications. *8 Mile* doesn't care to mention that the spoofing of racial and class identity is something that black performers have done all along. It nevertheless assures us that, when practiced by a white person, self-parodies of class and race become the stuff of heroic on-stage confessions.

Presented as a sanctimonious rite of passage, Rabbit's (and, of course, Eminem's) finding of whiteness enables him to appropriate a black art form with impunity. Instead of emulating corporeal blackness, he turns blackness into a darker shade of pale. As far as his art is concerned, he has infused rap with a metaphorical darkness quite specific to his own kind of whiteness—the whiteness of 'white trash.'

Black rap music has proven a vast enough field to absorb Eminem's variant without being eclipsed or getting distracted from its own concerns; it has even been generous enough to grant Eminem an official place among its own. In this light it is troubling that *8 Mile*'s protagonist, after he has 'found' himself and embraced his own blue-collar identity, suddenly no longer feels the need for black friends. When Future offers him a spot as a cohost of the Shelter battles, he declines because, he says, he needs to do his "own thing." His friends, sensitive as they are, understand. They watch as he walks down the same neon-lit alley through which, after his disastrous stage debut, he had earlier fled. This time, however, he echoes the Western hero who, in splendid isolation, rides off into the sunset.

The manner in which Rabbit leaves his friends behind at the club encapsulates their broader function within *8 Mile*. Despite its honorable intentions, the film ends up exploiting the social reality of the inner-city black people it portrays. It turns them into profitable spectacle, while remaining silent on the causes of their oppression. At the same time, the film is openly hostile towards the *Ebony* magazine set, which it juxtaposes with Rabbit's white working-class identity.

That *8 Mile*'s politics of class and race are confused at best is a fact few seem to mind. That the film gets away with as much as it does is due in no small measure to that charisma of its star, whose anger and outrage appear to be second nature. The key conduit for conveying Rabbit's transformation from white boy to proud, angry white boy is, of course, his face. If the reaction shot didn't already exist, it would have to be invented for him. Incredulous, wide-eyed, his mouth half open, Eminem's face sucks up the character's daily humiliations and indignities like a sponge before its features contort into an outraged expression with which he spews his contempt back at the world. It's like a slow accelerating sado-masochistic cycle: in order to become hyperaggressive, he must first expose his vulnerable side—even to the point of receiving a few blows. In fact, self-victimization is the best guarantee for upping the ante—hence, his self-debasing tirade before the Shelter's audience.

Authentic as they may be, Eminem's facial expressions end up fulfilling two crucial functions: first, they conceal that Eminem's anger is largely self-generated. Before we have time to question the righteousness of his complaint, he's already pissed off about something else, something bigger. His performance passes itself off as a long chain of reactions, when it is actually a very shrewd, proactive strategy to push his audience into passivity and empathy. But there is a second purpose to this guise of merely reactive anger: it drastically widens his artistic license—to the point where he can turn up the vitriol of his rap lyrics—and get away with it. In this sense, the way Eminem uses his face is perfectly analogous to the way rap music in general seeks to defend itself against charges

ROY GRUNDMANN

of hate speech and (however unjustified) demands for censorship. Rap's defense goes along the lines of, 'We don't create hatred—we simply *rearticulate* what's already out there.'

This attitude clearly identifies the Eminem phenomenon as a symptomatic response to the more recent politicization of ethnic, gender, and sexual minorities. While a natural talent such as Eminem can appear—and prevail—at any moment in pop-music history, his phenomenal success must be considered at least in part a belated reaction to the liberal pluralism of the Clinton era, during which minority politics became a school subject and minority representation increasingly seeped into entertainment and media. In a climate in which liberals kept singling out white male heterosexuality as a big bugaboo (even if they were white male heterosexuals themselves) a figure such as Eminem had tremendous appeal for those who also felt a need to complain but were, unfortunately, lacking any sort of platform. This type of sociological argument, however, fails to fully account for Eminem mania. He remains of interest, at least for now, not only because he embodies all of rap's contradictions (and particularly those of a white rapper) in fascinating manner, but also because he matches them with a similarly uncanny talent for combative poetry.

THE EMINEM CONSENSUS

Why We Voted for Slim Shady

by Richard Goldstein

from *Village Voice*,
November 13 - 19, 2002

two events of lasting significance occurred last week: the breakdown of the Democratic party and the breakthrough of Eminem. His debut film, *8 Mile*, became the highest-grossing movie in America just days after Republicans won control of Congress. These two events may not seem related, but they both reflect the mainstreaming of ideas that seemed extreme just two years ago. Bush's right-wing agenda and Eminem's violent misogyny were once considered over the line. Now they have crossed over and *become* the line.

Not that Em is a Republican (though he might favor ending the estate tax). But he and George W. Bush do have certain things in common. Both draw their power from the compelling image of the strongman posing as the common man. Both played the populist card to win the nation's heart. And I would argue that both owe their success to the sexual backlash.

When Scott Silver, whose last movie was *The Mod Squad*, was asked by Universal to write a screenplay for Eminem, he couldn't resist. "I pitched something that reflected [the] outrageous humor and cartoonish violence of his records," Silver told *Entertainment Weekly*. "They were like, 'Uh, no.'" Universal wanted to expand the demographic of its hottest music property, so Silver was ordered to create a drama that could reach an audience with reservations about Eminem. Bush faced a similar task in winning over an electorate with doubts about the economy. His solution was to play down the message and play up personality. *8 Mile* does something similar by associating its star with root values like struggle and community. It's a stump speech for Eminem.

Though *8 Mile* is being described as a blue-collar inspirational in the tradition of *Rocky*, it's more like a classic war movie with a white alpha male and an interracial unit. In this spectacle of the street, the sun never shines and the nights are tinted lurid blue. It's the perfect setting for a film about male combat and solidarity. All evidence that women play a powerful role in working-class society is repressed. The good bitches help their men; the bad ones betray them—end of story. Worst of all is our B-boy's dissolute mother. There's no attempt to reckon with the reasons for her haplessness. The social context is reserved for the men. They are full-blown characters; the women are full-bodied foils.

This distortion would have been noticed just a few years ago. But as the backlash advances, it gets harder to argue against the flattening of women without being pounded with the cudgel of p.c. A lot of men—and women—like it that way, at least in bed. It sure beats sex-role anxiety. What's truly alarming is the extra-libidinal dimension of this fantasy. There is growing pressure on women to cede their autonomy, and last week's election hinted at the result. The gender gap, which played a major role in recent elections, seems to have narrowed considerably this year. It's not just the reflex to close ranks behind the leader in a time of crisis; it's an impulse to stand by the Man. Bush benefits from this retrenchment, and so does Eminem, as the large female audience for 8 *Mile* attests.

Women are not the only swing constituency that voted in great numbers for Eminem. Many liberals are drawn by his populist aura, which 8 *Mile* plays to the hilt. Of course, populism is a two-edged sword: It validates the working class, but it can also justify the confinement of women to traditional roles. In most populist epics, men represent the people and women express solidarity. This, too, is a reassuring image, one that can reconcile many liberals to the backlash because it makes the sexual order seem progressive.

Liberals are no less susceptible than conservatives to nostalgia for a world where male power seems righteous, especially when it's allied with the truth-telling vitality of the street. 8 *Mile* is a feel-good movie with precisely that scenario. It kindles the old liberal dream about class trumping race while repressing the real reason why black and white men can bond over a rapper like Eminem. He gives them a common enemy: women. In fact, gender trumps *both* class and race in his music, but populism lets liberals pretend otherwise.

You wouldn't know from 8 *Mile* that bitch bashing is what made this angry white male a star. On-screen, our hero gets violent only with nasty dudes, and he's a friend to homos, chastising his posse for taunting a gay member. So much for Em's bad old boast about stabbing "you in the head, whether

RICHARD GOLDSTEIN

NOISE

you're a fag or lez." The willful forgetting of what these words actually mean is a sure sign that the social climate is changing. Eminem is an icon of that shift.

When Elvis Presley was ready for his close-up, he chose a historical romance with the buttery title *Love Me Tender*. It was an ideal crossover vehicle because it sublimated his sexuality into devotion. But the image onscreen was still Elvis of the writhing hips and sly regard. The audience could enjoy his transgressive aura while pretending to watch a love story. The same process of turning funk into frisson is now being applied to Eminem, but the times are very different now. El ushered in a sexual politics of Dionysian ecstasy and male display. Em emblematizes an age of sadistic pleasure and male control. In order for liberals to enjoy this show, they must convince themselves that something else is going on. This is where pop critics come in. Their job is not to deconstruct the culture but to preside over guilty pleasures.

frank Rich, the Times critic at large, certainly knows how to go with the flow. As the Eminem consensus evolved, so did he.

Two years ago, Rich described our hero as "a charismatic white rapper [who] trades in violence, crude sex, and invective roughing up heterosexual women, lesbians, and gay men." A year ago he pondered whether "racial crossover in the cultural market makes up for a multitude of misogynistic and homophobic sins." Now he's slamming "moral scolds" for dissing Em, while confessing, "I've been fascinated by him ever since I first heard his songs at the inception of his notoriety." Now Rich accepts the dubious claim that *faggot* is just "an all-purpose insult," and he regards the sexual violence as no worse than "typical multiplex Grand Guignol." Imagine the word *kike* becoming a generic insult—would that make it less anti-Semitic? Imagine racism as violent as the sexism in Em's oeuvre—would anyone slough it off as a charade?

You can claim, as Rich no doubt would, that the playa/ho dichotomy is just a metaphor in the service of arousal. But erotic fantasies are never just about sex. They are subversive precisely because they have the potential to construct a social norm. What does it mean when our most powerful public reveries are dedicated to male dominance and female submission? This is the crucial question posed by the triumph of Eminem—one most critics won't touch. Instead, they ratify the consensus, making it legit. Male dominance, the populism of fools, becomes something to celebrate. And when culture is on the same page as politics, you've got hegemony.

CROSSOVER DREAM

by R.J. Smith

from *Village Voice*,
November 6 - 12, 2002

In the money scene of 8 *Mile*, the young white Detroit rapper Rabbit Smith (played by young white Detroit rapper Eminem) battles a series of black MCs for the night's crown. We watch him find his game face in the mirror of the men's room of a club called The Shelter, then stalk the cement halls in a quick flip of *Gladiator*'s script. We watch him pull up his hood, psyching himself for the combat ahead. And when our hero hits the stage, the unlikely has been achieved. We feel sorry for Eminem.

He faces race baiting, flowing vast and volatile. The audience is overwhelmingly black, the badass competition is black, and they let him know what he is. The invective builds to what's got to be an explosion—race is about to burn again in a perpetually combustible city. That's what a movie that finally says race doesn't matter sets us up to think, anyway.

Two rappers get 45 seconds each to dismantle their opponent. A battery of push-button disgrace notes are hit. First up, Eminem is called "Elvis," but we'll let that one slide because it's so damned obvious, you know? (Scott Silver, 8 Mile's screenwriter and previously the director-co-writer of The Mod Squad, must have composed that one.) "Nazi," he's next called. Now we're cooking. That's pretty awful—Rabbit running with the Third Reich, the competitor raps, solely because he's the white enemy.

"Vanilla Ice," his opponent hits him within the next verse. If there's anything worse than being hated, it's being a clown. Say what you want about Hitler, the guy knew what "word to your mother" meant.

Trying to bump Rabbit off once and for all, the enemy now brings out his weapon of mass destruction. He's wearing a wife-beater, and he's beefy enough to make the words hurt just by flexing. "Beaver Cleaver," he calls Rabbit. And of all the things the white kid is labeled, it's this one he confides to his black sidekick that most got to him. Being hated, being a fool, hey, life's real rough. Whatev. But being called middle-class, and from a happy family—you can't let shit stand and still call yourself a man.

The only guys who truly play the race card are the evil posse called the Leaders of the Free World (hello Hollywood!), led by a rapper named Papa Doc (Apollo Creed was already taken). In the final round of the battle, Rabbit wails back, exposing Papa Doc as an alum of an elite suburban private school. That coup de grâce garrotes Beaver Cleaver and rips out Papa Doc's tongue. Rabbit owns the crowd, the city, the night.

Behind all in 8 Mile (see J. Hoberman's review) is the notion that class trumps race. If you are the white Rabbit living in a trailer home just beyond city limits and you want to get respect on the microphone, you have to take your lumps same as the homeboys in the ghetto. But if you are good, the movie says, your talent and sincerity will win out. The homeboys will know your name.

How is Eminem as an actor? Better than Sinatra in *Robin and the 7 Hoods*, worse than Sinatra in *The Manchurian Candidate*. Worse than Elvis in *Jailhouse Rock*, better than Vanilla Ice in *Teenage Mutant Ninja Turtles II*. Better than Madonna. On the one hand, when that mechanic-from-Hamtramck nose fills the screen it's hard to see him getting romantic lead parts. On the other hand, the guy has a hard look in his eye that would kill an iceberg.

8 Mile's flimsy script is made interesting by a good director and a charismatic star. What makes it important, maybe, is its belief that race doesn't matter. Working the stamping plant during the day, hanging with an integrated and uniformly motley crew at night, Rabbit is at home in the company of his fellow impoverished. The movie doesn't just provide the trailer trash; it shows the rusty septic tank behind the trailer. Race, it says, is exploited by those who stand to gain from dividing the masses—leaders of the free world, MCs looking for an edge. Hunger defines all: It generates realness and wins over a skeptical house.

"*grow up in detroit* and you understand the way of all things. Early on, you are put on close relations with entropy." So writes ex-Detroiter Jeffrey Eugenides, in *Middlesex*. His novel's narrator is a local misfit who struggles to understand his/her sexuality. The decaying city is the perfect backdrop for a divided soul's inability to come to rest. Eugenides continues: "As we rose out of the highway trough, we could see the condemned houses, many burned, as well as the stark beauty of all the vacant lots, gray and frozen. Once-elegant apartment buildings stood next to scrapyards, and where there had been furriers and movie palaces there were now blood banks and methadone clinics and Mother Waddles Perpetual Mission." That's the Motown captured vividly in *8 Mile*, a place ever imploding, and ever revealing more intense colors. For me and anyone else from Detroit, one scene will have special resonance: Rabbit's crew torches one of the hundreds of abandoned homes that dot the city. They dance around the urban ruin, chanting a hip-hop classic: "The roof's on fire." (The only thing wrong with this picture is that within three minutes you can hear the sirens. In Detroit they'd have time to chant the whole damn album.)

The road in Detroit named Eight Mile is layered with meanings. It was an early surveyor's landmark; it's the border dividing the chocolate city from its ivory suburbs to the north. The MC5's "Borderline" could have been about it; Ted Nugent claimed he could smell Patti Smith's B.O. from across Eight Mile's eight lanes.

In 1974, after the city had elected Coleman Young as its first black mayor, he dropped some science that terrified those in the suburbs. "I issue a warning to all dope pushers, rip-off artists, and muggers. It's time to leave Detroit—hit the road. Hit Eight Mile Road." Sensitive suburbanites claimed he was inviting criminals to invade their brand-new neighborhoods, and they did everything they could to isolate the city and keep those abandoned buildings ablaze. On both sides of the divide, Eight Mile Road became the racial crossroads, albeit a crossroads strewn with strip clubs and party stores.

Even before there were any trailer parks, the city nurtured those who longed to cross boundaries. In 1863 a full-on race riot erupted after a man thought to be white was "unmasked" as African American, and charged with sexually assaulting two women—one white, one black. The man, Thomas Faulkner, was memorialized in this 19th-century rhyme scattered by a writer who signed his name "B. Clark Sr., A Colored Man."

Now it be remember'd that Falkner [sic] at right
Although call'd a 'nigger' had always been white,
Had voted, and always declared in his shop,
He never would sell colored people a drop.

He's what is call'd white, though I must confess,
So mixed are the folks now, we oft have to guess,
Their hair is so curl'd and their skins so brown,
If they're white in the country, they're niggers in town.

To which a viewer of *8 Mile* might add, "If they're white from the trailer park, they're black after dark."

Up to now the genius of Eminem has been for short-circuiting understanding, for spotlighting the basic rhetorical rules we agree on—and then refusing to play along. You cannot disentangle his words, life, or art from one another. Sometimes he really means what he says and sometimes he's playing a part, and woe be to the outsider who can't tell the difference. Hate criminal, Bigfoot, latchkey kid, he's as much a product of the environment as any pop star could be, a great and useful monster to have on hand these past few years. But getting *that* person across in a movie wouldn't be easy, or likely to generate mega profits for the studio. So we get the latest version of crossover dreams.

At least Eminem's comfortable in front of the camera. Comfortable, that is, playing himself—or, bizarrely, a rewritten, reductive, and whitewashed version of himself. The general coordinates are in place—trailer home, Detroit, etc.—but the script crucially blanches the details. This is hagiography that takes advantage of a large audience to recast its hero. Eminem has been known to wave guns at foes on street corners; Rabbit pointedly barks at a buddy to put his gun away on a street corner. Eminem curses out his mother and says she's dead to him; Rabbit protects his mom when her boyfriend pushes her around. Eminem utters homophobic epithets; Rabbit sticks up for a gay guy singled out by another rapper. Eminem gulps down 'shrooms and purple pills; Rabbit has his head screwed on pretty well. Eminem learns to market his rage; Rabbit learns to control his. They have taken a question mark and turned him into a logo.

imagine entertainment honcho Brian Grazer may have got the project going, Curtis Hanson gave it a reason to exist, and Eminem brought it to life, but one more auteur hangs out in the background: 8 *Mile* co-producer and Interscope co-chairman Jimmy Iovine. Eminem gets under Iovine's skin. In recent years Iovine has declared white culture is over, and taken it as something of a mission to explain how race is receding as a marker of identity. Eminem is his proof that America is changing—he's not an Elvis figure, the record maker explains, because Elvis never got the kind of props in the black community that Eminem receives. Today "it's about class, not race, and hip-hop is one of the reasons," he recently told the *L.A. Times*.

You have to wonder if Iovine would be saying this if he didn't have Limp Bizkit and Eminem on his label, two white, hip-hop-influenced platinum acts. Or if he didn't know he was just playing charades—race is talked about all the time, while class distinctions remain taboo in a country where politicians excoriate those who "talk class warfare" and where everybody calls themselves middle class. Bringing up race can be bad for business—especially if you're white in the hip-hop world—while talking up class is a winner's game because absolutely nothing is at risk.

This gloss on race doesn't fit the real Detroit, the backdrop that keeps breaking through 8 *Mile*'s frame. The city is a product of race politics, a place where whites bailed after riots in 1967 and left a black power structure without resources to maintain a city. It's starting to shake off decades of entropy, but color-blind it isn't and shouldn't be. How many first-run movie theaters exist within city limits? One. Maybe the producers could have built a multiplex set, and then left it behind.

Twenty years ago, 8 *Mile* director Curtis Hanson's career took a big step forward when he co-wrote *White Dog* with the late Sam Fuller. That movie was a grieving, pessimistic piece that suggested we were all doomed to racial violence. However far the country has come since then, Hanson's come even farther—now he seems to believe we've overcome.

Too bad Fuller wasn't around for 8 *Mile*. It takes one race-obsessed anarchist mofo to know one. The old geezer would have slung so much bullshit back at the MC that Eminem's head would still be spinning. He'd have made a much tougher, more complicated movie, one that might have actually struck the sort of terror in the heart of America that the real rapper has. And he might have wrestled with the unexamined irony at the center of 8 *Mile*: how a white kid could find himself in rap, and then use the music both to fit into the black city, and to help him escape its grasp.

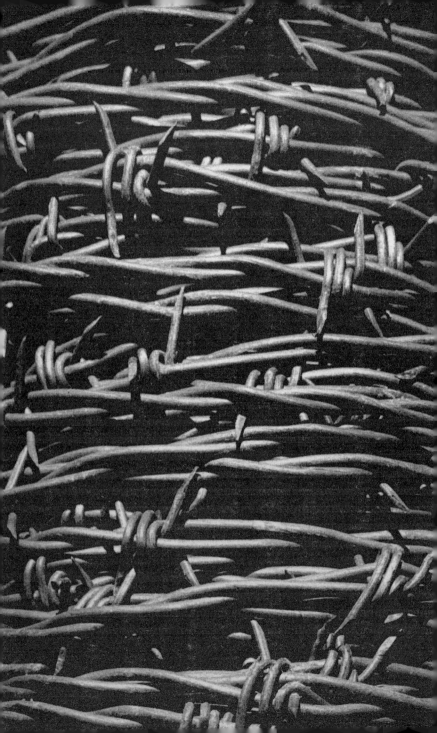

WHAT EMINEM MEANS—AND DOESN'T

by Robert Christgau

from *Los Angeles Times*, 2001

eminem's *The Marshall Mathers LP* begins with a statement of principles read by an announcer, the climactic sentence of which has gone strangely unremarked. Pardon me for sacrificing scansion and flava to the asterisk god as I quote it in full: "Slim Shady is fed up with your s***, and he's going to f****** kill you."

Without question this is a mortal threat directed at anyone who hears it. Bye-bye to all seven million Americans who have purchased the Grammy-nominated CD. Luckily for the future of profundity, few of the solons clamoring for Eminem's expulsion from the temple of civilized discourse are in danger, because they don't listen to Eminem—they just read about him. Still, moral arbiters agree that it's a bad thing to kill anyone, even teenaged hip hop fans. So why do you think I'm being silly? Because Hitler himself found killing that many people a logistical nightmare? Because Slim Shady is a fictional creation who can't kill anyone? Of course not—the reason's much simpler. It's because you don't think Eminem means it. So now let's figure out whether you think he means anything else.

Granted, that is to demand from the Eminem controversy a clarity it rarely achieves. Obtuse and uninformed though his critics may be, they're aware that his songs aren't pure acts of advocacy. With Marshall Mathers's fraught relationship with his real-life wife adding clear-and-present piquancy to the hand-wringing, there's generally reference to the rapper's violent "fantasies," his homophobic "epithets." The feeling seems to be, however, that Eminem's audience of unformed minds isn't up to such fine distinctions, and that his juvenile/sociopathic/exploitative/yucky self isn't either. Surely that's why "Janie Runaway" has gone unremarked in the current Grammy brouhaha.

You'll find "Janie Runaway" on another nominee, Steely Dan's *Two Against Nature*. It's sung in the voice of an aging pedophile trying to set up a threesome with his jailbait houseguest and a friend of hers. This being Steely Dan, the tone is complex, but that just means the pedophile isn't presented as a beast. I ask you, are aging males attracted to underage females less likely to kid themselves about their own morality than young men enraged at their female sexual partners? Will "Janie Runaway" help? As a critic who's the father of a 15-year-old daughter, I'd say there's more chance it will titillate. And as critic and father I nevertheless insist that "Janie Runaway" is a brilliant song.

But Steely Dan are in their fifties—now evolved, by the strange alchemy of respectability, from Rock Band Named After Dildo into Serious Artists. Eminem is a 27-year-old white practitioner of a genre that 20 years on was recently accused by anti-Eminem *New York Times* columnist Bob Herbert—a good left-liberal African American, so he should know—as having "thoroughly broken faith with the surpassingly great, centuries-long tradition of black music in America." Which is why I doubt hearing the music would tip the balance for many Eminem bashers. If you hate hip hop, then of course you hate Eminem. You probably aren't too fond of Lauryn Hill, either.

Yet how else is Eminem to be judged? This is the first major white practitioner of a sophisticated, foul-mouthed, "ill" aesthetic designed to give middle-aged blacks like Herbert conniptions—although, confusingly, his defenders rarely nail his precise achievement. Despite "Stan," about a crazed fan, or "My Fault," about a woman who OD's on Slim Shady's 'shrooms, he's not so much a "storyteller" as a rhymer; although no name rapper has done so much with enjambment and polysyllabic line endings, many are more poetic in other ways. Both his sound and his delivery privilege treble over bass, a pop strategy that leaves hip hop's core project of complex new beats and textures to deeper musicians. In short, he's a gifted technician, not a titanic one. But he's the funniest rapper ever. No rapper has ever made clearer, especially to young whites who view black rappers as romantic outlaws, that hip hop is a verbal construct, not to be taken literally. And no rapper has ever done so much with the fine distinctions that are supposedly over his audience's heads. It's not, as is too often said, that his artistry justifies his offensive content. His offensive content is the essence of his artistry.

Schooled in the over-the-top insults of the dozens, blaxploitation flicks, and slasher movies, the everyday brutalities of police harassment and the drug economy, and the early legal battles of 2 Live Crew and Ice-T, hip hoppers love reality games. They regularly boast about "keeping it real," and

regularly defend their tales of mayhem as fictions. Don't think Eminem is the first rapper to play with multiple personas, either. Still, Marshall Mathers the man, Eminem the artist, and Slim Shady the alter ego are an exceptionally well-defined trio deployed with exceptional intricacy, an intricacy hip hop fans are trained to comprehend. Rather than attributing his antisocial impulses to Slim and letting that be that, Eminem insists—gleefully, guiltily, perversely, thematically—that these subjective realities overlap.

It's fair to charge that Eminem and his music are homophobic, not simply on the basis of the vile but arguably contentless ritual epithet "faggot," but because various bawdy details corroborate it. But even his homophobia is examined by hip hop standards; "There's no reason that a man and another man can't elope," he concludes—from the examples of bestiality and cannibalism. And his "misogyny" is much more so. It's stupid or deceitful to argue that "Kim," in which you hear him slitting his wife's throat, is an incitement to murder. The wrong listener can misconstrue anything. But the unbearably raw pain of Slim's/Eminem's/Marshall's drunken rage, misery, and insanity render "Kim" a far more socially responsible work than "Janie Runaway." The teenagers know what the moral arbiters don't understand.

Two tracks later comes the finale, "Criminal," where Eminem supposedly threatens to murder "a fag or a lez." Only he doesn't. Explicitly and unmistakably, there for any person with a 90 IQ to understand, the song is about *words'* power to cause pain. It too comes with a statement of principle, uttered by Eminem himself. It's about how "stupid" it is to think he'd kill anyone "in real life." It concludes: "Well s***, if you believe that, then I'll kill you."

Think he means it? I f****** hope not.

EMINEM— BAD RAP?

by Richard Kim

from *The Nation*, March 5, 2001

does *The Marshall Mathers LP*—in which great white hip-hop hope Eminem fantasizes about killing his wife, raping his mother, forcing rival rappers to suck his dick and holding at knife-point faggots who keep "eggin' [him] on"—deserve Album-of-the-Year honors? This is the question before members of the National Academy of Recording Arts and Sciences (NARAS), who have, since nominating Eminem for four Grammy awards, received unsolicited advice from a bizarre constellation of celebrities, journalists and activists ranging from Charles Murray to British pop singer (and Eminem collaborator) Dido.

Bob Herbert of the *New York Times* took the opportunity to deplore not just Eminem's lyrics but the entire genre of rap music for "infantile rhymes" and "gibberish." In a more nuanced report, *Teen* magazine asked, Eminem: angel or devil? and discovered that 74 percent of teenage girls surveyed would date him if they could. The Ontario attorney general even attempted to bar Eminem from entering the country for violating the "hate propaganda" section of the Canadian Criminal Code.

But the most vociferous and persistent criticism of Eminem has come from an odd combination of activists: gay rights groups like the Gay and Lesbian Alliance Against Defamation (GLAAD) and family-values right-wingers like James Dobson's Focus on the Family. They all argue that Eminem's album threatens not only the objects of his violent lyrical outbursts but also, in GLAAD's words, the "artist's fan base of easily influenced adolescents who emulate Eminem's dress, mannerisms, words and beliefs."

In the face of all this attention to Eminem's "hate speech," even the usually taciturn NARAS is doing some public soul-searching. The academy's president, Michael Greene, recently said, "There's no question about the repugnancy of many of his songs. They're nauseating in terms of how we as a culture like to view human progress. But it's a remarkable recording, and the dialogue that it's already started is a good one."

As I have been forced to sit through all this Eminem-inspired hand-wringing over the physical and psychological well-being of faggots like myself, I've wondered just how good that dialogue really is. For one thing, so much of what has been said and written about Eminem has been political grandstanding. For example, Lynne Cheney, not usually known as a feminist, singled out Eminem as a "violent misogynist" at a Senate committee hearing on violence and entertainment. Eminem's lyrics, she argued, pose a danger to children, "the intelligent fish swimming in a deep ocean," where the media are "waves that penetrate through the water and through our children...again and again from this direction and that." Pretty sick stuff. Maybe it comes from listening to *Marshall Mathers*, but maybe it's the real Lynne Cheney, of lesbian pulp-fiction fame, finally standing up.

GLAAD, for its part, argues that Eminem encourages anti-gay violence, and it has used the controversy over Eminem's lyrics to fuel a campaign for hate-crimes legislation. While GLAAD and Cheney have different motives, both spout arguments that collapse the distance between speech and action—a strategy Catharine MacKinnon pioneered in her war against pornography. Right-wingers like Cheney and antiporn feminists like MacKinnon have long maintained such an unholy alliance, but you would think gay activists would be more cautious about making such facile claims. After all, if a hip-hop album can be held responsible for anti-gay violence, what criminal activities might the gay-friendly children's book *Daddy's Roommate* inspire? Because the lines between critique and censorship, dissent and criminality, are so porous and unpredictable, attacking Eminem for promoting "antisocial" activity is a tricky game.

Thankfully, GLAAD stops short of advocating censorship; instead it asks the entertainment industry to exercise "responsibility." GLAAD launched its anti-Eminem crusade by protesting MTV's heavy promotion of *Marshall Mathers*, which included six Video Music Award nominations and a whole weekend of programming called "Em-TV." After meeting with GLAAD representatives in June, MTV's head of programming, Brian Graden, piously confessed, "I would be lying to you if I didn't say it was something we struggled with." Liberal guilt aside, MTV nonetheless crowned Eminem with Video of the Year honors and then, in an attempt to atone for its sins, ran almost a full day of programming devoted to hate crimes, starting with a mawkish after-school special on the murder of Matthew Shepard, called *Anatomy of a Hate Crime*, and concluding with a seventeen-hour, commercial-free scrolling catalogue of the kind of horrific and yet somehow humdrum homophobic, misogynous and racist incidents that usually don't make it into the local news.

Perhaps understandably, Eminem's detractors still weren't satisfied, but given the fact that Eminem is one of the best-selling hip-hop artist of all time, what exactly did they expect from MTV and the Grammys but hypocrisy and faithless apology? And what do they really expect from Eminem—a recantation? Does anyone remember the homophobic statements that Sebastian Bach of Skid Row and Marky Mark made a decade ago? Point of fact: Marky Mark revamped his career by becoming that seminal gay icon, the Calvin Klein underwear model, and Bach, long blond locks still in place, recently starred in the Broadway musical *Jekyll and Hyde*. All of which just goes to show, if hunky (and profitable) enough, you can always bite the limp-wristed hand that feeds you.

Meanwhile, the dialogue among Eminem's fans has been equally confusing. Some, like gay diva Elton John (who's scheduled to perform a duet with Eminem at the Grammys) and hip-hop star Missy Elliot, praise Eminem's album as hard-hitting reportage from the white working-class front. They argue that his lyrics are not only excusable but laudable, because they reflect the artist's lived experiences. This is, as London *Guardian* columnist Joan Smith pointed out, a "specious defence." Should we excuse Eminem because he is, after all, sincere? Should we ignore his own genuinely violent acts—like pistol-whipping a man he allegedly caught kissing his wife? Others, like *Spin* magazine, have defended him as a brilliant provocateur. Far from being about realness, they argue, *Marshall Mathers* is parody, a horror show of self-loathing and other-loathing theater, a sick joke that Eminem's fans are in on. They point to how he peppers his rants with hyperbole, denials and reversals, calling into question not only the sincerity of his words but also their efficacy. For example, he raps about how he "hates fags" and then claims he's just kidding and that we should relax—he "likes gay men."

I don't know if Eminem really likes gay men, although I'd sure like to find out. What is clear from listening to *Marshall Mathers* is that he needs gay men. When asked by MTV's Kurt Loder about his use of the word "faggot," Eminem said, "The lowest degrading thing that you can say to a man when you're battling him is to call him a faggot and try to take away his manhood. Call him a sissy, call him a punk. 'Faggot' to me doesn't necessarily mean gay people. 'Faggot' to me just means taking away your manhood." Of course, using the word "faggot" has this effect only through its association with homosexuality and effeminacy, but there, really, you have it. Homosexuality is so crucial to Eminem's series of self-constructions (he mentions it in thirteen of eighteen tracks) that it's hard to imagine what he would rap about if he didn't have us faggots.

Eminem is, in his own words, "poor white trash." He comes from a broken home; he used to "get beat up, peed on, be on free lunch and change school every 3 months." So who does he diss in order to establish his cred as a white, male rapper? The only people lower on the adolescent totem pole than he is—faggots. This strategy of securing masculinity by obsessively disavowing homosexuality is hardly Eminem's invention, nor is it unique to male working-class culture or hip-hop music. Indeed, Eminem's lyrics may be more banal than exceptional in the way they invoke homophobic violence.

Marshall Mathers reworks the classic Western literary trope of homosexuality, which manifests itself as at once hysterical homophobia and barely submerged homoeroticism. It reflects the kind of locker-room antics that his white, male, suburban audience is well acquainted with. So too were Matthew Shepard's killers, Aaron McKinney and Russell Henderson, and the perpetrators of the hate crimes MTV listed (who were, not so incidentally, almost all white men), and, for that matter, the Supreme Court, which recently held in the Boy Scouts' case that homophobic speech is so essential to boyhood that it's constitutionally protected. Herein may lie the real brilliance of Eminem as an artist and as a businessman. In a political culture dominated by vacuous claims to a fictive social unity—tolerance, compassionate conservatism, reconciliation—he recognizes that pain and negativity, of the white male variety in particular, still sell.

So does *Marshall Mathers* deserve Album of the Year? Well, I probably wouldn't vote for it, but if it does win, that would be perfectly in keeping with Grammy's tradition of rewarding commercial success. And where might a really good dialogue on homophobia, violence and entertainment begin? It might look at why *The Marshall Mathers LP* proved to be so pleasurable for so many, not despite but rather because of its violent themes. It might start by seeing Eminem not as an exception but as the rule—one upheld not just by commercial entertainment values but by our courts, schools, family structures and arrangements of public space. As Eminem says, "Guess there's a Slim Shady in all of us. Fuck it, let's all stand up."

THE KIDS ARE ALRIGHT

by Hank Stuever

from *The Washington Post*,
February 18, 2001

this one goes out to anyone whose parents ever said turn it down.

Which is almost everybody. What are you doing in there? Well, turn it down. The ancient rift.

Now it's now. "This is one of the best songs ever," Jeff Kim is telling me. It's a Wednesday afternoon and we are in his suburban Maryland bedroom, which he keeps neat: plaid bedspread, Orioles posters, rubber numchucks from martial arts lessons. He is cueing up a CD, "2001" by Dr. Dre, in his mind an incontrovertible classic; I am bracing myself. He skips over several tracks—"Xxplosive" and "Still D.R.E."—and stops before "Let's Get High" and "Bitch Niggaz."

Jeff is 14 and in the eighth grade. He hits the Play button

on the Aiwa stereo on top of his dresser. I put my chin in my hand and listen. Off we go.

A duet between Dre and his cohort Eminem: "So [bleep] ya'll all of ya'll," Dre raps. "If ya'll don't like me, [bleep] me. Ya'll are gonna keep [bleepin'] around wit me, and turn me back to the old me."

The beat is slow, accompanied by a synthy-string sound, but the message rolls faster than you could ever register it on a cold listen. It's a song about how Dr. Dre feels he isn't valued enough by . . . whom, exactly? Other rappers. His critics, "haters." An indeterminate other.

Eminem handles the chorus (and there is one): "Nowadays everybody wanna talk like they got something to say, but nothin' comes out when they move their lips, just a buncha gibberish. And mutha[bleepahs] act like they forgot about Dre."

"This is the best song?" I ask, when "Forgot About Dre" ends.

"Everyone likes this song," Jeff says. "You hear it everywhere you go. They retired it on 'TRL.'" ("TRL" is "Total Request Live," MTV's daily Nasdaq report of heartthrobs and hits.) "Haven't you heard it?" Jeff asks me. "You had to have heard it. In our school, if you didn't know this song . . . wow. I think you would have to think twice about the person who didn't know this song. You'd think, that boy's got problems."

(I don't know this song.)

(Clearly I have some problems, which I think about a lot lately. One of the problems is that I woke up and the world had changed, which I suppose is everyone's problem, sooner or later.)

I ask Jeff: "What's the saddest song you can think of?"

"The saddest song?"

"Yes, like when you're unhappy about something. What would you listen to?" Maybe it's the wrong question. Jeff isn't sure if he ever gets that unhappy.

"I guess 'Stan' by Eminem."

"Then play 'Stan' for me."

He cues up the CD, Eminem's Grammy-nominated "Marshall Mathers LP." Again, I brace myself. Most of what I know of Eminem is what I've read, as a full-fledged grown-up, as that cranky, abstract adult we never think we'll be. Eminem is disqualifying me from partaking. He makes me say this one terrible sentence, aloud, to teenagers no less: These songs all sound alike.

"That's what my dad says," Jeff says. "This one is different. My mom likes this one, I think because of the melody."

"Stan" is Eminem's rap about a fan gone out of control, who writes him letters, waits hours for him to sign autographs, and finally becomes so obsessed with the singer that he kills himself and his girlfriend. Against a repetitive R&B dirge sung by a female voice, Eminem rails against anyone who would love him too much.

I've had the bizarro-world Eminem logic explained to me, deconstructed and theorized upon, backward and forward: Eminem doesn't mean those awful things he says about people, especially homosexuals and women. (Then why does he say it?) Eminem is just taunting his critics. (Which critics exactly? The press seems to love him, except for the occasional unamused op-ed columnist, whose sphere of influence on eighth-graders, we must assume, is limited.) Eminem wouldn't really kill his wife, like he says he would. (Fine. Would he just at least say one nice thing about her?) Eminem is a master comedian, true ironist, rapping about what's on everyone's mind. (Um, Eminem raps mostly about his own career, and how hard it is to be Eminem.)

"I feel sorry for Eminem, in a way," Jeff says as the song ends.

"I think I do, too," I say. "But probably in a different way."

"He just wants to be himself," Jeff says. "He just wants everyone to leave him alone."

Finally I get it, almost in a flash. You have to go into the bedroom of a 14-year-old boy to understand. Leave me alone is a refrain I remember. Leave me alone has broad and ultimate appeal. It happens to inform our Bill of Rights; it's about nobody understands me; they don't understand us; I just wanna be me. "What are you rebelling against?" they ask Marlon Brando in "The Wild One."

"Whaddya got?" Brando says, from his motorcycle.

The eternal echo of pop.

So ugly it is of course beautiful.

You can kill a thing like Eminem by loving him too much, by understanding him. You can give him a Grammy and make him sing a song with Elton John.

This seems to be the plan.

Sometimes we become the music we listen to, or it becomes us.

For a while it's hard to tell.

A toddler seems to like your Eric Clapton; then it goes wrong. Your house thunders with bow-wow-wow-yippy-yo-yippy-yay and the strangest kinds of screams; you think the Devil is being born upstairs. When does it start spewing split-pea soup? You mumble to yourself: Alice Cooper, Alice Cooper, Alice Cooper. (Alice Cooper used to seem like the end of the world, a man named Alice, of all things, done up like some effete demon, singing a song about tearing up the school. Now it's now; he seems quaint. See how everything really does blow over?)

Pop is accidental and irrepressible, which is why they sometimes call it infectious. A disease you don't mind having. Years later something forgotten comes on the radio and you'd like to pull over and just sit there a minute, alone. Someday perhaps they will reminisce about "Thong Song," by Sisqo: "Baby move your butt, butt, butt . . . "

Here is Lauren Williams.

We are sitting in her bedroom playing CDs for one another on the boombox she has owned since the fourth grade. We are playing some of the songs that make her sad, and then some of the songs that make me sad. Some of the songs that changed her life or make her think about love; then some of mine. Her bedroom window looks out over a cluster of town houses in Columbia, and bare February trees.

Lauren is 15, a sophomore at Wilde Lake High School, which is in the Village of Wilde Lake, set in a world of grassy knolls and streets that sound like the stray stanzas of bad poems. In her earliest memories, there is Michael Jackson. It turns out his music is to kids today what nursery rhyme songs must have once been to other generations. He is Mister Rogers, Jesus and Barney. Michael Jackson's greatest hits is the first CD Lauren bought with her own money.

In fifth grade, maybe sixth, there was a boy who liked Nirvana. But one day the angst dried up, Lauren says, and the music she was listening to had become "too complicated." She took the hormonal antidote: boy bands.

"You have to understand," she says with a stunning clarity, pushing her soft brown bangs away from her eyes, "If you were ever a 14- or 15-year-old girl, you would find it very easy to be taken in by the sounds. You know it's crazy and you don't want to stop. It's cultlike. You don't have to stop. You're supposed to love them."

Which is how she found herself standing in Times Square last March with hundreds of girls, all screaming up toward the plate-glass windows of MTV's studios, while the band 'N Sync arrived to promote its latest album.

The sound of teenage girls screaming. Did they remember to put it on that space probe that left the solar system? Would aliens understand?

Something changed again. The heartthrob music got "too

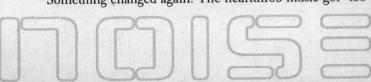

simple," she says. "It's just a pattern you go through. Pretty soon you want depth again." She has scraped away most of the boy-band pictures from her bedroom walls, except up high, where she can't quite reach. Tiny pieces of Scotch tape remain; a blank stretch of paint awaits something new. Her room has matured. It feels like something harder, more obscure, is about to come on.

There is a boy she liked, but he graduated last year.

It was a crush, she says, not a romance. "It was one-way." It was just the act of seeing him walk by in the halls. Here is a song about it, by a band called Jamiroquai. She puts it on.

All I want to do is spend a lifetime with you, baby.

Make it happen.

Eighteen thousand years ago: In the eternal months just before all of us got driver's licenses, we had to traverse the suburbs by intricate carpool arrangements, and we always argued about the radio. Def Leppard would come on, singing "Photograph," and we'd say, ooh, turn it up. ("I see your face every time I dream, on every page, every magazine.") Duran Duran brought some debate. ("Her name is Rio and she dances on the sand.") "They're fags," said our future alpha male, a football player, and who could protest? (Who'd dare?)

Finally we would sit and say nothing, knee-against-knee in the back seat, staring out the windows and listening to the music, writing on each other's hands with ballpoint pens.

All the way to school, that horrible, gorgeous pop music would wash over us, sung by suggestive androgynes: So now I come to you with open arms, hoping you'll see what your love means to me. Sweet dreams are made of this, who am I to disagree? Do you really want to hurt me, do you really want to make me cry? Owner of a lonely heart, much better than an

owner of a broken heart. I've got it bad, got it bad, got it bad—
I'm hot for teacher. (She blinded me with science and hit with
me with technology.) I guess I must be dumb, because you had
a pocket full of horses—Trojan, some of them used.

I wonder if our parents listened.

I knew a girl whose mother once, and only once, broke the
adult laws of carpool and sang along with a song on the radio.
The song happened to be a big hit by the Pointer Sisters; it
went with an Eddie Murphy movie and ultimately became
the kind of vacuous thing you'd hear in sports arenas during a
lull. "I'm just burnin'," the carpool mother sang, "doing the
Neutron Dance."

She turned it up and sang as loud as she could, sang as if
mortified teenagers were not in the car at all, a screeching
falsetto. She pulled up in front of the school, dropped everyone off, and sped away.

"Your mom is hilarious," I said to the girl.

"I hate my mother," she said.

We are each born of a neutron dance.

Tiny particles of infinitesimal mass and influence, with
radios in our bedrooms, waiting to be absorbed into pop culture's hungry nuclei, which dazzlingly and subliminally tell
us to get away from our mothers and fathers and whatever
music they listen to. Music splits us, and puts us back together. Get a freak on, get it on, bang a gong, show that thong.

We are swept into the malls of America and then spat out
into oldies-format demographics as if we never existed. Some
of us move from apartment to apartment with milk crates of
vinyl records and warped cassettes that we never play. We
keep bumping into nostalgic versions of ourselves. We hire
deejays to work at our wedding receptions and give them spe-

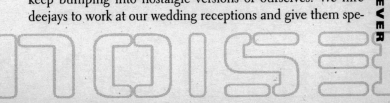

cific orders: Please play "Love My Way" by the Psychedelic Furs. Please play "Shower the People" by James Taylor. Please play "I Want You to Want Me" by Cheap Trick and "More Than a Feeling" by Boston. Please play "In My Life" by the Beatles.

We ask this from the bottom of a hole called uncool.

The death of the stereo: This will be the first generation to think twice before taking a stereo system to their college dorm rooms, or beyond. Even after the copyright issues play out, they'll want their hard drives instead, where they store music like gathered bits of string, a pop nest.

The death of liner notes: They keep their CDs in little Mylar zipbooks. Sometimes they throw the original case (the "jewel box") and liner notes away. Long gone is the notion that you lie on your bed, wearing Princess Leia-bun-size earphones, and trip out on the elaborate LP cover art. (Curiously, rappers have entire pages of homeys to thank, which nobody reads.)

The death of music as home decor: Smaller, hidden, compacted, put away. Farewell to the space-age bachelor with his prominent walls of albums and CDs, his speakers the size of file cabinets, the fetishizing of things like woofers and tweeters; witness the death of audiophiles, who could never do what these kids do to bass controls.

The death of the full-length album: The rise of the single track. Delete the songs you don't like, reshuffle them in any order.

The death of record stores: "It's a waste of time," Chris Hall, a senior at Wilde Lake, tells me. "You can get what want a whole lot faster, without having to look for it."

The death of goofing off in record stores: See above.

The death of the homemade mix tape: But never fear, ye

lovelorn, for there is now the self-burned CD. (Such a great verb, burn. Look how I burn for you. Listen how I burn for you.)

What remains: Groupthink, thank God. The hits are still the hits, because if they weren't, we'd also see the death of hysteria, obsessions, slamming doors, posters torn from magazines, class reunions.

The written use of the English noun "teen," referring to an age group, is by one account just 328 years old.

In the spirit of remediation, I bought the Dr. Dre CD at a Sam Goody music store in Columbia Mall and listened to it over and over, mulling its bitches, its niggaz, its hos, its many mutha[bleepahs].

I drove around the pleasant subdivisions with Dr. Dre in my head and tried to imagine hearing it at a dance. You know, a dance. With crepe paper streamers and balloons. (Is there still crepe paper? Do they still put up balloons? Am I insane to want to know this?)

"I knew a girl named Nikki, I guess you could say she was a sex fiend," sang Prince, in 1984, when I was in high school. But I don't think we ever played this song at a dance: "I met her in a hotel lobby masturbating with a magazine."

These are a few of the lyrics that sent Tipper Gore to Capitol Hill with such fervor—a fervor that, to some degree, must have embarrassed her own teenager at the time. One of the end results of this ruckus was the "Parental Advisory— Explicit Lyrics" sticker that's on just about any new CD owned or coveted by the middle- and high-schoolers I met in

Howard County. The stickers seemed irrelevant to the parents. Maybe Tipper was a genius. Maybe she was Chicken Little. Will the butt dance ruin civilization? Will "Thong Song" spell our doom? Archaeologists will decide, if they can reconstruct a Walkman.

In a year I'll leave the latter fringe of the 18-34 demographic, which is the entertainment industry's most charitable and lucrative extension of the eighth-grader in all of us. None of the music I like comes with Parental Advisory stickers and I guess this is my way of knowing I've died. I'm supposed to go quietly.

It's a kind of trap. If you say the Backstreet Boys and 'N Sync are just pale imitations of the Spinners or the Jackson 5, then eventually you're going to have make good on that claim. You put on the Spinners record and realize from the first notes that you've already lost the fight. The Spinners sound spare, only half as in love as today's boy bands. Your version sounds anemic. Their version sounds thick, robust, young. Your records can let you down.

Take the Ramones and the Clash. You find yourself lecturing some kid about how much Blink 182 owes to the Clash. Acting on this, I played parts of the Clash's 1979 album "London Calling" for Jeff Kim, in his bedroom.

While I was watching his face, the music suddenly sounded different to me: It sounded like it was played by people who were sitting down. I played more songs. He was horrified by Jimi Hendrix ("Let me stand next to your fire," Hendrix sings. "Oh," Jeff says. "Hmmm. No, this is wrong." To him it sounded too real, too plain—a man playing drums, a man playing guitar, a man playing bass. Nothing there, no sex, no flow, no rage.) Pop tunes from the '80s remind him of being in a grocery store. The Go-Go's sound like a cartoon.

For a while, I was undaunted. I saw it as my role to deliver, like an adjunct professor of VH1 Studies, a brief synopsis of the history of the rapper wanting to kill his bitch ho:

"Well, see, this is classic for the male protagonist facing infidelity. It's like Hendrix already sang 34 years ago: 'Hey, Joe, where you goin' with that gun in your hand? I'm goin' down to shoot my old lady,' and so forth, which, in turn, takes us back to the blues . . ."

Snore.

Is there anything more boring than a rock-and-roll museum?

And has anyone told this to the people who are building rock-and-roll museums?

I hung out one evening with James McNamara, who is 18 and a senior at Wilde Lake High School and happened to write a college application essay about the sad commercialization of music. He knows there is the pop music that will define his high school days, and then there is what everyone else would call real music. Driving to school, he listens to opera (Puccini) or classical music (Ravel). He plays jazz on the piano, writes his own songs. I sit and listen.

"What's the saddest song?" I ask him. "What would you put on the CD player if you were feeling sad?"

"Hmm," he says. "There's some really evil Mozart. There's opera, they all die." Then he decides on "Kind of Blue" by Miles Davis. "If you're elated, it can sustain the elation, but if you're depressed, it's in there, too. There's so much in every note."

James's mother brings out cookies, hot tea, trophies he's won for music, his portfolio of drawings. There was always music in the house, Led Zeppelin, the Beatles, Aaron Copland. One day

James began playing jazz riffs on the piano. "My dad says, 'Hey, write a pop song and make a million dollars,' " James says. "Like this?"

Here his hands change; the song he was playing on the piano goes perky. "It hurts me to play it."

That said, he fully expects to hear "Thong Song" at his high school reunion. He would want them to play it.

The kids let me into Clarksville Middle School in spite of the fact that I cannot sing "Forgot About Dre." It is a Friday morning, and Jeff Kim and some of the other eighth-graders sit in a classroom and cheerfully try to tell me whatever happened to music.

There are Matt and Jessicah and Randi. There are Greg and Patrick and Chris and Megan and Jeremy. They can all agree that popular music is "a little bit better" now than it has been in the past.

But what of the future? What will their own children listen to?

"I will let my kids listen to anything," Greg Mazur says, "Except country." (Almost guaranteeing the fates will supply him with a child who loves country music.)

"Or a song that says 'Kill all the parents,' " Jessicah Midy says.

"Or if it's against God or something," Jeff says. (God is faring pretty well amid the foulest language of today's pop. Rappers almost always thank Him first in their acceptance speeches, then sing of slashing ho's.)

Greg likes some of what his dad listens to, except jazz. "My dad has been buying all these jazz CDs. It's horrible to me. It's just random noises."

"My dad has, like, all these Billy Joel records? I think he

has all of them?" says another boy toward the back of the classroom. "It's the worst thing you ever heard."

"Like with the Beatles?" another boy says. "Um, okay, I like the Beatles? Because you can hear what they were trying to do? But they didn't have the technology, sort of, to do it the way they could have done it now? Like the beat is there? But something is kind of missing? I don't know, like it doesn't flow the same?"

If you were Megan Hedrich, you would hear the Backstreet Boys and that would be the sound of slow dancing. It would be the sound of all that intimacy that girls always think is happening to everyone else but them. It wouldn't really matter to you that it doesn't meet anyone's standards of good music. If you are a boy, in Limp Bizkit you hear the adrenaline, almost like the perfect expression of the way your blood chemistry feels, how it is changing. As the rappers Jay-Z and Ludacris puff themselves up and scream, the children of Howard County and everywhere else hear friendship, togetherness, understanding.

"Really?" I say. "I know this is going to sound wrong, but when I hear this kind of rap, I start to think someone is about to get beat up. Probably me."

"It relaxes me," Jeff says.

i go to Randi Engel's house one day after school. It's several winding roads away from Jeff's, on a street called Empty Song Road. I tell Randi's mother that the story is about what music her daughter and her friends might be sentimental for in 20 years, and why.

"Isn't it a shame that none of it's any good?" her mother says, cheerfully. She grew up on Springsteen, FM hits. Randi's father doesn't like her music, "at all—he thinks it's noise. But it's okay because it's not like it's changing my personality," Randi says. There's a CD player in the basement, so we decide to sit down there.

When she was a sixth-grader, she says, she used to talk on the phone to her boyfriend. She'd play him songs by boy bands and he would make gagging sounds. He played rap songs for her, and they stuck. She leans now toward acts like DMX, Ludacris, Jay-Z.

The boy bands are over and done for Randi, except when she's thinking about boys. "When I'm having a guy problem, that's the best kind of music." ("My Everything" by 98 Degrees for example. "It's a dream-guy song," she says. "A good-looking guy expressing himself, how it feels, how he feels. But that won't ever happen, right?")

Earlier she had mentioned "Butterfly" by a band called Crazy Town. "That's the CD I have to get," she says.

I pull the Crazy Town CD, newly unwrapped, out of my bag. I went and bought it on another reconnaissance mission to Sam Goody. It has a Parental Advisory sticker, so I'm not going to give it to her, but let's listen. "They're more rock, like Limp Bizkit." She puts it on, and starts dancing. Her mother comes downstairs to clean out a closet and take out some trash. "Mom, this is the CD you have to get me," she says.

"Butterfly" is a groove. "Come my lady, come come my lady, you're my butterfly, sugar, baby." It goes on:

Such a sexy, sexy pretty little thing
Fierce nipple pierce you got me sprung with your tongue ring
And I ain't gonna lie cause your loving gets me high
So to keep you by my side there's nothing that I won't try.

"This song is the best," Randi says.

"It's about sex," I say.

"Right now everything is about sex," she says. Teenagers have always had that peculiar ability to convince you that the music is harmless, or that it's not really about them. "If it gets too sexual you can't listen to it," Randi says. "You don't want to. If it's about sex, does that mean it's going to make people have sex?"

I shrug.

She shrugs.

It is Randi who confirms for me that there are still dances, and there are still moments when you want a boy to ask you to dance, and either he does or doesn't. When the eighth-graders' favorite songs are played, the adult deejay dutifully plays the version without the four-letter words, which the children supply by screaming out in unison during the gap of silence.

Randi told me that her friend Greg Mazur "has a lot of good music," so I go to his house, a few streets over, the next day. Greg is wearing long cargo shorts and a bright red T-shirt. He listens to the closest thing today's teenagers have to old rock, minus the concept-album gravitas, laden with influences of punk and rap. He listens to the Deftones, Rage Against the Machine, and thinks he might be the last boy in the world who likes Metallica.

Once, when he had to write a report for a reading class, he wrote about the Dead Kennedys, a 1980s punk rock band that the snob in some of us would call seminal, though that may be stretching things. Still it's gratifying: Somebody still cares.

"He gets it from his dad," Greg's mother, Sherre, says. This is a perfect pop house: They exposed the baby to a proper diet of rock and blues. Greg shares, with his father, Glen, a love for Led Zeppelin and Pink Floyd. One will impatiently wait for the other to finish with the computer so he can download more music.

Then they went different ways, because 50 years of popular-music consumption practically insists on it: father toward jazz, son toward . . .

"Slipknot," Greg says.

"Slipknot?" I ask.

"That's something my dad cannot stand."

"Play it," I ask.

He jumps up and puts on a song called "Wait and Bleed." I brace myself, yet again. "I wander out where you can't see," a man sings. "Inside my shell I wait and bleed." It's fast and hard-driven but has a kind of beauty to it, and I cannot understand it, and it just may be the prettiest thing I've heard lately. I want to jump up and down. I make a note to myself to return to the mall and buy it. How quaint, buying a record. At the mall.

And when I do, it doesn't sound the same in my car.

Somehow I knew it wouldn't.

Swarms of children on Razor scooters fly down steep driveways, through the empty songs.

This goes out to anyone who heard a song and knew it was about them.

Curtis Gore, a football player at Wilde Lake High School who usually listens to Jay-Z ("Parking Lot Pimpin'," say, or "Streets Is Talking") to sustain the euphoria of his existence, tells me there is one song so sad he thinks he can no longer listen to it. "What is it? What's the saddest song?" I ask him, figuring I wouldn't know it.

"Amazing Grace," he says.

"Wow. That's a great answer," I say. "That might be the best answer. Do you put it on when you feel sad?"

"I did," Curtis says.

He had heard the song a few weeks earlier at the funeral of a friend who was shot at a party. A day or so after the funeral, he came home from school and put the song on, in his bedroom. He lay down and listened. Halfway through he stopped it.

"I couldn't take it," he says. "So I opened the file and I deleted it."

NOISE

WHY EMINEM SHOULD GET THE GRAMMY

by Whet Moser

from *salon.com*, February 21, 2001

eminem's Grammy-nominated album, "The Marshall Mathers LP," clocks in at 75 minutes. That's almost as much music as you can fit on a single CD. With his "Songs in the Key of ADD" style, it's a lot of words.

Yet the Detroit rapper has spawned a dialogue that dwarfs the album, in size and occasionally in vitriol. And for all the trees that have been sacrificed for the sake of the critical battle that has raged as the Grammys approach, neither his defenders nor his detractors have produced much that history will remember.

Instead, Eminem has received the most banal, reactionary responses. Hipper-than-thou music critics mostly like him, but they miss the point. And the feel-good (or at least feel-self-righteous) posturing from gay advocacy groups like GLAAD *and* Lynne Cheney is even worse. What both groups are unwilling to say is that "The Marshall Mathers LP" is a searing, complex, whirling, grotesque work, and the most deserving Grammy nominee in years.

The chances of Eminem actually getting the record of the year award are roughly nil. (It's doubtful he would have been nominated were it not for new rules that allow a sort of super-committee to override the members' embarrassing nomination omissions.) The work is far too extreme for the National Academy of Recording Arts and Sciences. To vote on the Grammys you have to be a professional record-maker in some capacity—and a member of NARAS. Despite some outreach campaigns in recent years and occasional, almost accidental recognition of an important artist or two, the group is still overly influenced by the old-school worlds of classical and bland pop.

The music critics are almost uniformly right: This is a great work, and Marshall Mathers/Eminem/Slim Shady is a huge talent. Dr. Dre's production is typically adamantine—beats and vocals hit hard. Eminem's irresistible hooks and chants stick in your head. And the rapper's sheer verbal power marks every song with off-kilter rhymes, in-jokes, contradictions and insults.

Unfortunately, they've been right for all the wrong reasons. Most of the early reviews called the record a "guilty pleasure," or pointed out particularly sharp references or jokes. One Eminem slam, directed at Christina Aguilera and Carson Daly of MTV's "Total Request Live," was reported nearly everywhere.

The rest of the time, the critics have tried to explain away the most obvious parts of the record: its misogyny and its homophobia. Take this, from Dimitry Leger in last week's *Village Voice* annual Pazz & Jop Critic's Poll, which called "The Marshall Mathers LP" the fourth-best record of the year:

"Eminem didn't hate more fags or promise to kill more bitches on his latest album than the average credible gangsta rapper does per verse. Critics who fail to hold black rappers to the same moral standard will henceforth appear to be on some very uncool and outdated shit."

The most irritating rock-crit tendency—the desire to appear risky even though you're 27 and have an M.A. from Brown—was replayed in almost every review. Worse, the tone of these reviews was almost always halting, begrudging, guilty or pained.

And sometimes, the criticisms were painful themselves. At what might have been the lowest point of the yearlong Eminem controversy, Michael Greene, president of NARAS, wrote a dense, blockheaded defense of the album's status as "the voice of rebellion."

This is odd. "The Marshall Mathers LP" is not a pleasant listen. The music is little more than a mnemonic device, its halting, spare beat the perfect complement to the rapper's irritating persona. He's the high school classmate from hell. To use that oft-repeated verse, Eminem resorted to attacking lite pop music with "shit, Christina better switch me chairs/So I can sit next to Carson Daly and Fred Durst/and listen to 'em argue over which one she gave head to first." Any hip-hop fan would recognize that the line is not particularly offensive, particularly trenchant or particularly funny.

When the album is not being tragic and scary, as in "Kim," the song where Eminem imagines killing his ex-wife (again) and "Stan," where he talks to an obsessive fanboy, it's just being dumb. Eminem admits as much, in "The Real Slim Shady," the album's most popular song:

I'm like a headtrip to listen to Cause I'm only giving you Things you joke about with your friends inside your living room The only difference is I got the balls to say it in front of y'all And I don't gotta be false or sugarcoated at all

Well, maybe *you* don't. But maybe you did. Or you know, or live with, or were raised with or went to school with someone whose idea of humor is:

At 13 I was putting shells in the gauge on the shelf I used to get punked and bullied on my block Till I cut a kitten's head off And stuck it in this kid's mailbox ("I'm Back")

Maybe there is a little Slim Shady in all of us. I know there is in me, and I suspect there is in you.

I live in a rural county outside Roanoke, Va., the "Star City of the South." My grandmother's house, in nearby Lynchburg, is a five-minute walk from Jerry Falwell's. This is the region where Appalachia borders on the South, and Roanoke is significant for being the cultural and financial center of a famously poor, backward region. As a reasonably wealthy railroad town between historically downtrodden cultures, it's also a remarkable mix of traditions, ideas and classes; a fascinating study in the vast divides between people.

I went to a small alternative school in the city. Because it discouraged competition, I had to play county sports, where, three seasons a year, there was more than a little Slim Shady in everyone around me.

The Roanoke Times, the local newspaper, recently ran a four-part series on being gay in Roanoke. They were essentially sympathetic but hardly strident pieces, making a plea for tolerance mostly through the example of nonjudgmental observation.

The series was met with a torrent of criticism from people appalled that the paper would defend tolerance. The newspaper ran a follow-up piece addressing the reaction. An editor wrote:

Many readers, though, said they would have been happier with no stories at all.

"Roanoke is a conservative town," one woman said. "To dedicate the number of pages to the gay lifestyle is disgusting."

Other readers said the series painted a false picture of the Roanoke Valley. They said it made Roanoke appear more accepting of homosexuality than it truly is, and they worried that the stories would attract more gays and lesbians to the region. Some even worried that it would drive away residents offended by the gay lifestyle.

Welcome to deepest, darkest America. It's this America that Eminem, in the tradition of great Southern realists such as Dorothy Allison, illustrates vividly and accurately. This aspect of his art is the one that most of his critics, in their rush to gain the moral high ground, have missed or ignored. "The Marshall Mathers LP" sheds a scary light on a phenomenon both rural and urban, Southern, Northern and American: for lack of a better word, white trash.

His critics accuse Eminem of making this, um, lifestyle cool (a charge given an ironic credence by fawning rock critics). Yet he's much smarter than that. You don't have to have a degree in semiotics to recognize that an album with three multilayered, untrustworthy narrators—Eminem, Marshall Mathers and Slim Shady—can hardly be charged with the straight-up advocacy of *anything*.

Anyone waiting for the real Slim Shady to stand up is going to be there awhile. If you missed this in giggling about Jennifer Lopez impregnation fantasies, however, he also shows a humane side. In "Stan," a beautiful song that reads like a good short story, he writes to a fan:

And what's this shit you said about you like to cut your wrists too? I say that shit just clownin' dawg, c'mon, how fucked up is you? You got some issues, Stan, I think you need some counseling To help your ass from bouncing off the walls when you get down some

Or, more pithily:

> A lot of people think . . . That what I say on record Or what I talk about on a record That I actually do in

real life . . . If you believe that . . . Then I'll kill you
("Criminal")

Here he's doing what he does best—calling people out.
He's as bad as you imagine him to be.

Yet we have every right to be scared by Eminem. We're not
worried about rock critics and essayists abusing their girl-
friends because of this album, any more than we're worried
about Yale students reading the Marquis de Sade. We're worried about dumb people listening to this album. And we
should be. If Eminem doesn't scare you, visit some of his fan
sites. On antimusic.com, Mechelle writes:

"Eminem is the bomb. If you agree you rock. To all ya out
thiere that hate him, you suck peoples penis! you guys are gay
pussys! hes the hottest mother f*cker out there!"

She signs it, "Peace."

Two types of people listen to Eminem. There are some
who appreciate his language and narrative as it should be
appreciated: as good literature. There are also those who think
his darkest manifestation, Slim Shady, is someone to be emu-
lated. As many albums as he's sold, both types obviously exist
in droves. I'll leave it to your personal balance of optimism
and pessimism to decide just what the percentages are.

This is where his genius lies. "The Marshall Mathers LP"
succeeds in the manner that truly great art should always succeed. First, it describes a problem—and not in the distanced,
pleasant way that, say, Arrested Development does (or, rather,
did).

Second, it proves the problem is real, scarily real.
Significantly, it does this as much through album sales as it
does through language.

Finally, it has the guts to terrify people, to get people mad.

But if there's a problem here, it's us. The people with the
reason, education and humanity to fix the problems that

Eminem writes about are more interested in fixing him. Rather than concentrate on devastating income gaps and a shoddy educational system, his critics—on both the left and the right—would prefer he tone down the darkness that is essential to the effectiveness of his work, or shut up altogether. And because no one will go far enough to suggest that he be banned or otherwise restricted, none of this really amounts to anything at all.

This is why he deserves record of the year, and any other Grammys he doesn't give a damn about: because it will piss people off. As Zack de la Rocha of the late, great Rage Against the Machine put it, "Anger is a gift," and our anger is Eminem's gift to us. It's not as if the Grammys have ever been in touch with the most important or even the best records since, oh, Bobby McFerrin won an armful of statues for "Don't Worry Be Happy."

Eminem is most likely not going to win record of the year. But the awards are still a barometer of the music industry, if not popular culture or good music. This year, in the record of the year category, NARAS has a number of choices before it. The members could honor Radiohead's "Kid A," which is sufficiently arcane and audience-unfriendly to be art; Paul Simon, for making, in "Still the One," the thousandth or so pristinely produced album of his career; Beck, for making "Midnite Vultures," the best party album in, oh, a few months; Steely Dan's "Two Against Nature," an arch collection of state-of-the-art jazz-pop songs; or Eminem, an artist of immense social significance and creative talent, the only artist in the crop who is taking real risks, who is standing up and telling society something that it truly, genuinely doesn't want to hear.

In his first album, Eminem—rather, Slim Shady—claimed "God sent me to piss the world off." I'm starting to believe it.

GENIUS – NOT!

Eminem Melts in Your Hands

by Armond White

from *www.firstofthemonth.org*

a knowledgeable hiphop lover's list of the best rap artists would not include Eminem, the 30-year-old white rapper (born Marshall Mathers III) from Detroit. Lacking Scarface's sonority, Chuck D's vision, Biggie's fluency, L.L. Cool J's flair, Slick Rick's humor, Jay Z's brilliance, Ice Cube's astuteness, Rakim's flow, Ice-T's roguishness, Flavor Flav's ingenuity, Snoop Dogg's slyness, Eminem's critical acclaim is due not to vocal virtuosity or verbal mastery. Instead his endorsement by the mainstream media has everything to do with the spectacle of whiteness. Even some black rap fans participate in this adoration; they're grateful for white attention to a black cultural form, even when the goal is to expropriate it. Eminem's assertion of underdog status—imitating the black rapper's stereotyped vitriol—actually works to reinforce racial myths that separate whites from blacks. That's why Emimen—and not the rappers mentioned above—has been acclaimed a genius.

Eminem appropriates styles of speaking and behaving that white pop audiences have coveted since Norman Mailer's 1958 essay "The White Negro" brought race-envy out of the closet. This was confirmed last summer when *The New York Observer* asked oldster journalists Paul Slansky and Janet Maslin for testimonies to the white rapper. Soon after, the *Village Voice*'s Robert Christgau raged against a colleague, Richard Goldstein, for calling Eminem homophobic. Goldstein dared to challenge Christgau's (and the media industry's) coronation of Eminem as "a genius."

Eminem's songs deflect attention from the inequalities that derive from racial oppression. Never identifying with blacks, he avoids expressing solidarity with the frustrations black rappers feel. And that's not simply because his experience as a white suburbanite is different; his industry triumph depends on asserting the privilege of being white in America—the prerogative to whine about petty shit while leaving one's "brothers" behind.

It is this malcontent's style of white rap—as opposed to the good-time rapping of Vanilla Ice, Beastie Boys, 3rd Base, Kid Rock—that reinforces racial polarization. Eminem limits hiphop's usual themes (songs that variously recall the tradition of social protest from Negro spirituals and Civil Rights era agitation) to mere juvenile griping, trashing rap's political potential while connecting to the triviality of corporate pop. This has been praised as Eminem's "rock move," an assessment that (in its very reliance on rockist attitude) only mystifies social and cultural difference. Anthropologists agree that race is an unscientific concept, but rock critics won't admit that Eminem's swaggering racial identity satisfies their own need for advantage over other people, citizens, artists.

Eminem has to be proclaimed a "genius" (the same way Christgau ordained P.J. Harvey a genius while never so honoring Mary J. Blige's musical expression of personal female dilemma) in order to sustain the group-esteem of whites. This mindset rules the major institutions of pop journalism (Eminem's *Vibe* and *Rolling Stone* and *New York Times* cover stories) and now the film industry (with the release of Eminem's mediocre movie *8 Mile*). Indifferent whites always thought rap was a sociopathetic art and Eminem's aberrant imitation seems to confirm their misperception. His belligerence is respected as if it came from a deeper hurt, a smarter head than those squabbling Negroes. None of this indicates the arrival of a great or innovative artist; it's the old story of racial aggrandizement—the pressure to distinguish one mischievous white from hiphop's horde.

Behind this white-as-genius charade is the notion that black artists live through their bodies not their minds—a prejudice that bebop fought against in the 50s and that hiphop should have countered definitively. In the 80s, it was explicitly disputed by the r&b-inspired postmodernism of white artists like Green Gartside, whose group Scritti Politti put an academic gloss on the musical structures and vocal expressions that were taken-for-granted (that is, considered un-intellectual) when employed by Aretha Franklin, Michael Jackson or Debarge. (Green's interviews, cover-art and studio collaborations with Miles Davis, Chaka Kahn, Marcus Miller were veritable footnotes citing black genius.) Despite the creative deconstruction and reflexivity in innumerable hiphop compositions, artists from Public Enemy to De La Soul, Son of Bazerk to Jay-Z have never received the commendations immediately heaped upon Eminem. Denying them praise is fundamental to racist hegemony. It implies that before Eminem there was no genius in hiphop.

This is how pop media works: There were too many Beastie

Boys to focus the same white-media admiration—plus, the over-celebrated Beasties weren't much interested in playing out the separatist overtones (after all, they're Reform Jews and Buddhists). But Eminem reaps the benefits of playing to white nationism. ("I never would have dreamed in a million years I'd see/So many motherfuckin' people who feel like me/ Who share the same views and the same exact beliefs . . . ") He emphasizes grievance without inquiring into its social/political roots—a method of rabble rousing as old as Dixie.

Love will bring us together, as fellow Detroiter Kid Rock knows, rising out of the Motor City's white working class with loud, funny tales of ambition and lust and black-white awareness. But the anger shtick keeps Eminem singular—a lightning rod not just for gay and feminist groups offended by the epithets and taunts in his lyrics but also for the subconscious resentments of empowered, "liberal" whites. Eminem's bitterness connects with their sense of entitlement and his rap venom unloads their hidden fear of losing power; giving them leverage (pop cred) against all those highly vocal, aggrieved young blacks who have previously commanded the cultural stage.

Thus Maslin's approbation: "A lot of what [Eminem] says makes me uncomfortable but the bottom line is if it's good you have to acknowledge that. And it is. It's very cathartic to listen to him." One wonders if Maslin felt catharsis from Geto Boys' "Still," Michael Jackson's "They Don't Care About Us," Public Enemy's "Nighttrain," Morrissey's "Nobody Loves Us"? Similarly uninformed, Paul Slansky says: "There should be no stigma attached to being an Adult who loves Eminem." Desperate to appear with-it, these middle-aged writers outdo the embarrassments of naïve young record-buyers who confuse Eminem's belligerence with brave truth.

No artist can be blamed for being what he is not, but when Eminem's unenlightened tirades are over-praised, his specious stance must be closely criticized. Rather than a figure of cultural resistance, he's the most egregious symbol of our era's selfish trends. With his bootstrap crap and references to rugged individualism reminiscent of the 80s, he's a heartless Reagan-baby—but without the old man's politesse. Unlike most black rappers, Eminem rejects fraternity and his hostility toward women (his mother and babymama in particular on the songs "Kim" and "Cleaning Out My Closet") betrays rap's usual call for social unity. His first single, "My Name Is" confessed a carefully calculated psychosis; Eminem's multiple personalities (including Slim Shady) conveyed the bewilderment of reactionary youth. His three albums of obstinate rants culminate in the egocentric track "Without Me," making him the Ayn Rand of rap—a pop hack who refuses to look beyond himself. On the song "White America," he asks "Have you ever been discriminated?" insulting blacks but shrewdly alerting his white-flight constituency. It suggests that Eminem speaks the feelings of poor, disenfranchised whites but that's mostly a marketing myth. I observed at an 8 *Mile* screening that his most enthusiastic audience are those middle-class, middle-aged whites reveling in the peculiar animus they feel towards Americans who might be gaining on them.

Eminem has become a star for exactly the reasons the media excoriates black rappers—his enmity and anger. Saying it's white folks' turn to vent, however, isn't the same as acclaiming this rapper—out of all rappers—a genius. That belittles rap as mere aggression. But minus righteousness, angry rap is dismissible. Rap is exciting when it voices desire for social redress; the urge toward public and personal justice is what made it progressive. Eminem's resurrected Great White Hope disempowers hiphop's cultural movement by debasing it. His "Soldier" gloms on to black rap's rebel posturing but its "controversy" and "playa hating" are clichés. It makes no original statement like Biggie's "Mo Money, Mo Problems" or Willie D's "I'm Goin' Out Like a Soldier." And nothing's duller than a pop star calling himself radical or complaining about being rich. "This is not a game this fame...No one ever puts a grasp on the fact that I sacrificed everything I had," Eminem says in "Say Goodbye Hollywood" (a tune more like Billy Joel's lugubrious ballad than L.L. Cool J's funny-rueful "Goin' Back to Cali."). How spoiled, how appalling!

"Cleaning Out My Closet" is even more petulant, with its draggy, flat final accent—a dull, mean flip of Tupac's "Dear Mama." There's no emotional development here, no compassion; it's a thoughtless, ponderous song. (As a black female BET comic said, "How you gonna teach your daughter to love by refusing to let her grandmother ever see her?") But reviewers overlook the pettiness of Eminem's attitude. "Imagine witnessing your mama poppin' pills in the kitchen," he raps. Less sympathetic than the Stone's "Mother's Little Helper" or "19th Nervous Breakdown," its cock-rock arrogance sets a new low in hiphop sexism. Malcolm McLaren's pioneering '80s Buffalo Gals project offered an affectionate example of cultural borrowing with ebullient female metaphors (and featuring ersatz do-si-dos sampled on "Without Me" and "Square Dance") but Eminem simply steals from McLaren and rejects his cross-cultural positivity. Even "Square Dance's" lyrical climax is lame and repetitive: "Nothing moves me more than a groove that soothes me/ Nothing soothes me more than a groove that boosts me/ Nothing boosts me more suits me beautifully/ There's nothing you can do to me/ Stab me shoot me/ Psychotic hypnotic product/ I gotta take antibiotic/ Ain't no body hotta and so on/ And yada yada gotta talk a lotta/ Humm de le le lada/ Oochee walla walla/ Hmm de dada dada/ But ya gotta gotta." Fact is, you gotta be ignorant of the past year of hiphop to think this is anything but derivative.

And his threat "to ambush this Bush generation" never rises to the level of the stinging political commentary in PE's cogent jibe "Son of a Bush." "Square Dance's" politics aren't radical or genuinely subversive—just a fretful rejection of any American authority. Not biting the hand that feeds him. It's mere spite. The sputum of a Ritalin kid.

When Eminem invites Dr. Dre, Nas, Busta Rhymes, to "come square dance with me," he inadvertently exposes white pettiness, inviting black rappers to join his pity party. Eminem's meanness overcomes no social obstacles and so must be heard differently from marginal voices that express exhaustion, effort, justified opposition. Boasting "I could be one of your kids. Little Eric looks just like this/ Erica loves my shit/I go to TRL/ Look at how many hugs I get," he enjoys both the censure and the money the white majority gives him. But he foolishly presumes he's the first pop star to fight for his right to be dirty/arty—"The ring leader of the circus of worthless pawns/ March right up to the steps of Congress and piss on the lawns of the White House/ To burn the flag and replace it with an advisory sticker/ To spit liquor in the face of this democracy of hypocrisy/ Fuck you Ms. Cheney/ Fuck you Tipper Gore/ Fuck you with the freedom of speech this United States of Embarrassment would allow me to have." Ice-T and Luther Campbell already made this argument. So did Twisted Sister. Yet Eminem's trite puns are supposed to pass for profundity.

He raps, "We sing for these kids who don't have a thing/ Except for a dream and a fucking rap magazine" as if pledging fidelity (keeping it real). But if he thinks capitalism works that simply—or answers generational despair so easily—then he's a worthless, deluded folk fraud, shilling for the industry instead of thinking his way through desperation. When Eminem shouts in "White America" about "a fucking army marching in back of me," the reference is to that stunning MTV Awards moment when scores of peroxide-blond white boys in t-shirts marched behind Marshall Mathers into Radio City Music Hall—a processional toward media coronation that was political as well as fashionable. A kid from militia Michigan should know such a "rebellion" humiliates democracy, rather than demonstrating its radical fulfillment.

It's awful to celebrate Eminem's juvenile manner, his inability to work through personal/political issues. On "Without Me" the line "This looks like a job for me" comes from superhero comic books but really just describes a money-making opportunity. Eminem's carpe diem lacks any feeling for the complex legacy of working class struggles, which should be familiar to any Detroit area resident. Springsteen did much more with work-life on *Darkness on the Edge of Town*. For Eminem, factory town life, trailer park life, white working class economic stress never even inspire a good, resonant couplet.

Speed rapping and over-rhyming instead, Eminem simply plays back music critics' praise: "Everybody only wants to discuss me/ But this must mean I'm disgusting/ But it's just me/ I'm just obscene/ Though I'm not the first king of controversy/ I am the worst thing since Elvis Presley/ To do black music so and use it to get myself wealthy/ Hey, here's a concept that works/ 20 million white rappers emerge/ But no matter how many fish in the sea/ It'll be so empty without me." Obviously, Eminem never heard Chuck D's caveat, "Don't rhyme for the sake of riddling." At least the song's la-la-la-la-la chorus is funny, blending with his whiney voice into a bratty update of early Beastie Boys. White critics love the mischievousness; it's a bourgie outlet. But let's be unfair for a bit and compare "Without Me" to an Hypnotic Biggie boast: "My car goes 160/

Swiftly/ Wreck and buy a new one/ Ya crew run run run/ Da doo run run" Biggie adopts the history of pop to portray his largesse, not squeezing rhymes into one pinched scheme but expanding the rhyme and rhythmic pattern. This is true genius rap and it gets better when Biggie slides into a fantasy pimp scherzo:

> Tell them hos,
> Take they clothes off slowly
> Hit em with a force like Obi
> Big black like Toby
> Watch me roam like Romey
> Lucky they don't owe me
> When they say show me
> Homie

The awesome, pop modernist range of Biggie's references cohere with the brevity and plausibility of the rhyme sources—*Star Wars*, *Roots*, Frank Sinatra, the street—without ever explicitly defining what comprises his fantasy world. It's sexual, criminal, historical, musical and, in the end, what Eminem never is: affirmative.

Isn't it time we stopped calling Dr. Dre a great producer and overlooking the odious content of his material? ("I lit a flame up under his ass," Eminem raps, making no mistake who the star is.) Anyone who's heard the production that Jay-Z, R. Kelly and Tone got on the dazzling but neglected *The Best of Both Worlds* cd (or recalls how Hank Shocklee, Prince Paul and Easy Mo Be redefined the art song and brought new vision to the concept-and-party album) would know that Dr. Dre has competition—if not superiors—in the game of beats, flow and thrills. He's done no production for Eminem that matches his work for Snoop Dogg, Blackstreet or Tupac and that fact underscores Eminem's lack of originality. Taking behavior lessons from drug-glamorizing, woman-beating Dr. Dre is bad business. Eminen conspires with Dre to promote the worst kind of cynicism in the 50 years of rock and roll's existence. You hear it most clearly in "Stan." Unlike the M&Ms candy from which Marshall Mathers took his stage name, this song is not sweet and it melts in your hands upon examination:

"Stan," Eminem's most celebrated track, folds an epistolary rap into a horrorcore scenario. Eminem begins by portraying an adoring but troubled fan whose letters get angrier when Eminem doesn't answer. (The fan locks his pregnant girlfriend in a car trunk and commits suicide.) Critics impressed by the song's turgid O'Henry coda had already fallen for Eminem's political con, his pretense of embodying the anxieties of white working class youth. Metal groups have told similar tales with more panache. There's merely self-pity in Eminem's version. (When he answers his fan with corny advice, it's too late). Dre gives Eminem a doomy soundscape, paced by samples of Dido's "Angel" that schmaltzes-up the fan/star relationship. There is plausible pathology here ("Sometimes I even cut myself to see how much it bleeds!") but the solipsistic, defensive braying has the same disingenuousness as Eminem's trailer-park demagoguery. In "Paint a Vulgar Picture" (1987) singer-lyricist Morrissey of The Smiths evoked the lonely working-class yearning that Eminem exploits by dangling the carrot of pop fame. Eminem distorts hiphop fans' enthusiasm whereas Morrissey understands the classic star/fan dynamic—his song is, by far, the greatest pop treatment of the way private desire becomes public and obsession turns into critique. Trivial in comparison, "Stan" appeals to American music critics (who were apathetic to The Smiths' ambisexual Brit pop) because it flows with their sense that male vanity is sacrosanct. Suckers for "Stan's" false drama, their readiness to cling to Eminem's machismo was an early sign that enthusiasm for him would be regressive.

Here, in "Stan's" quandary and desperation, we find the conventional power mechanism behind Eminem's straight white male spectacle. "Stan" coddles male insecurities that Morrissey queered by daring to offer a sensitive (romantic) insight that challenged rock's heterosexual hegemony ("In my bedroom in those ugly new houses, I danced my legs down to the knees") as well as record-industry greed ("Reissue, repackage...slip them into different sleeves/ Buy both and feel deceived"). Morrissey detailed heartbreakingly mundane pop experience while Eminem only sensationalizes and sentimentalizes it—a double-whammy which suggests he's cramped by a fear that empathy is weak, unmasculine. But that's precisely what makes Morrissey's perspective transcendent, subversive, humane.

The Pet Shop Boys' disappointing answer to "Stan" and Eminem's homophobia, "The Night I Fell in Love," also falls for Eminem's spectacle—unhelpfully eroticizing it as rough trade, a negotiation with conventional (and hostile) masculine symbolism. While their one-night tryst with Eminem can be heard to offer an embrace instead of censure, it's really a rare moment of The Pets painting a vulgar picture, succumbing to hegemony. Their song may be an object lesson in teaching-by-example, but Eminem, a revanchist cultural figure, represents a stubborn ideology. Christgau excused him by saying "The reason Eminem means more than the Pet Shop Boys at his best is how provocatively and passionately he [tests] the tension between representation and authenticity that's given rock and roll fans that funny feeling in their stomachs for nearly half a century." For some of us, that funny feeling is nausea.

The best hiphop narrates the journey of boys into emotional maturity. Goldstein's essay decrying Eminem's homophobia pointed to the acceptance of hiphop's backward turn. Eminem's tracks—unlike Morrissey's or The Pets'—pander to juvenile bad-boyness ("I write fight music for high school kids") in ways that anyone over 13-years old should see through. Hateful or ironic, his white Negro parody is not a purposeful ruse. In the silly "The Night I Fell in Love" The Pets are being pitifully forgiving—sissies—to ignore that real art is about sincerity. They endorse Eminem, wanting to be hip. Christgau and his ilk want to be young again and irresponsibly free to hate.

Eminem has started something more twisted and complex than ordinary ignorant behavior. He has perverted the way we perceive hiphop's history and promise through his degradation of everything the culture previously stood for. Randomly choose any pre-*Chronic* rap track—say, Ice-T's "Somebody's Gotta Do It"—and, despite the crass pimpology, the record exudes pleasure. Listen to the sounds, beats to wordplay; there's an expansive generosity you never hear in Eminem. ("'Yo, Ice, your homeboy Adnan Khashoggi called up; wanted to borrow some more money.' 'No problem! Small thing to a giant!'") For three minutes hiphop joyously redeems sexism, materialism, the whole rotten world. Eminem (screaming from his little cell in "hell") traduces hiphop's oppositional and affirmative roots—as did Dr. Dre's *The Chronic*. But this time the pop media makes sure that all benefits accrue to the standard figure of American power: a hateful, selfish, childish white male. The status quo, yo! When you hear Eminem get personal on "Hailie's Song" (dedicated to his daughter) it's hair-raising to realize how much enmity and pettiness he passes on—bequeathing emotional death to his own child, and marketing it to all America's children.

VOICE OF AMERICA

by Kelefa Sanneh

from **Rolling Stone**, July 24, 2003

remember when Eminem was only a rapper? it was just a few years ago. But since then, his records, videos and movie debut have made him . . . what, exactly? If you're looking for a precedent, you may find yourself fumbling with hypotheticals. What if Kurt Cobain had been a movie star? What if Madonna were a virtuoso? What if Tupac Shakur had been twice as popular—and blond?

It's not just a matter of numbers, although numbers matter. Eminem has sold 20 million albums, making him the top-selling rapper ever. At a time when most stars aren't selling what they used to, he remains the only sure bet in the music industry. *The Eminem Show* was the best-selling CD of 2002, *8 Mile* brought in more than $51 million in U.S. theaters, and its soundtrack moved 4 million copies. Even his business is booming; the year's most popular act, 50 Cent, is signed to Eminem's Shady Records.

It's partly a matter of skills; Eminem can rap circles around the competition. But it's also a matter of sensibility. Eminem is an extremist by inclination, but he also has a knack for tri-angulation, an ability to find a midpoint between seemingly contradictory impulses. His style is all hip-hop swagger and hard-rock self-loathing (can we call him the original angsta?), and he knows how to court pop fans by insulting them. In "Soldier," when he declares, "Never was a thug, just infatu-ated with guns," he is simultaneously asserting his hip-hop credentials and disavowing them.

Then there are the family ties. The rapper who raps like an angry kid is also a thirty-year-old divorced father of one, and Eminem is always reminding us how much he hates his mother and loves his daughter. If his songs sometimes sound like dinner-table monologues, that only heightens his appeal to disaffected kids who—as he likes to say—dress like him, act like him and feel like him. Eminem explains how it all works in "Sing for the Moment," where he imagines a parent's nightmare:

Walking around with his
headphones blaring

Alone in his own zone,
cold and he don't care

He's a problem child, what
bothers him all comes out

When he talks about his fucking dad walking out

*'Cause he hates him so bad
that he blocks him out*

*But if he ever saw him again,
he'd probably knock him out*

*His thoughts are whacked, he's
mad so he's talking back*

*Talking black, brainwashed from
rock and rap.*

But before he became a hero to crabby white teenagers every-where, and before his testy encounters with Moby and Triumph the Insult Comic Dog—before, that is, he decided that you catch more listeners with vinegar than with funny—Eminem was just another rapper doing what rappers always do: begging to be liked. Wasn't that the reason he invented Slim Shady in the first place? He wanted to entertain everybody. It's there in his rhyme flow, in the way he rants a mile a minute, trying to impress us all, like the most insecure guy at the party. Listen to "Just Don't Give a Fuck," where he calls himself "the looniest, zaniest, spontaneous, sporadic/Impulsive thinker, compulsive drinker, addict/Half animal, half man." He sounds as if he's just waiting for someone to offer him a beer and tell him to relax.

He probably wouldn't know how. Eminem is far and away the least laid-back hip-hop star ever, and overachievement has always been part of his appeal. His rise to fame began with a kind of audition—at the 1997 Rap Olympics MC Battle, in Los Angeles—and a few years later, he was still rapping like a guy who was out to win a competition. He won over Dr. Dre by freestyling on a radio station, so maybe he figured he could win over listeners the same way.

It was 1999 when *The Slim Shady LP* came out, and hip-hop was in full "crews-control" mode, thanks to the Wu-Tang Clan and Puff Daddy and Master P and everyone else. Rappers wanted to make us believe it was easy: Put together a big enough army and the money would flow in. By contrast, Eminem was on his best behavior, humble and hardworking. He wanted to be a famous rapper, like the ones he idolized— you could detect a trace of awe in "Guilty Conscience," one of the best songs from *The Slim Shady LP*, where he mocks Dr. Dre for being "Mr. N.W.A/Mr. AK-comin'-straight-outta-Compton-y'all-better-make-way."

He was good, even—or especially—when he was running his mouth off about how bad he was, ranting about how he had persuaded a college girl to experiment with drugs. Those dirty jokes were his way of proving his sincerity, and his enthusiasm. He was willing to do whatever it took.

In retrospect, it's hard to imagine a better way for the first great white rapper to make his entrance. For two decades, hip-hop had been awash in black stereotypes, and now Eminem was bringing two of the most infamous white stereotypes to life: He was both a crazyass white boy and a hardworking white man. He was nasty without being disrespectful, and his flow was as ridiculous as his videos.

If success made him uncomfortable then, it wasn't because he didn't like having fans but because he knew all the tricks he'd used to pull them in. And so, on *The Marshall Mathers LP*, he spent more than an hour assessing his own appeal. "Now, because of this blond mop that's on top/And this fucked-up head that I've got/I've gone pop?" Well, yes—wasn't that the whole idea? Whoever said that "Kim," his bloodcurdling wife-killing narrative, was an affront to women was missing the point. It was an affront to listeners. He was asking us, "Is this what you want?"

If Eminem's goal was to be accepted in the world of hip-hop, then his strategy succeeded and backfired at the same time. Anyone who was serious about hip-hop had to respect him, but his most enthusiastic fans were the people who saw him on MTV. He was doing all the things rappers are supposed to do: making records with Dr. Dre, filling his verses with unexpected rhymes and analogies, cursing up a storm, getting arrested. And yet the more Eminem acted like a rapper, the more he was praised for his individuality. People who had never paid much attention to brilliant black rappers such as Jay-Z and Rakim suddenly found themselves raving about Eminem's nasty stories, his rough reputation and even—when they really got carried away—his enjambment.

Obviously, a backlash was on the way, and *The Eminem Show*—clever and paranoid and hermetic—seemed to anticipate it, maybe even conjure it into existence. His success had been built on a deception: He was the rapper everyone loved to hate, and yet it was getting harder to find anyone who really hated him. His performance at the 2001 Grammys with Elton John may have been awkward, but it wasn't ineffective; after that, only his most fanatical detractors could still be bothered to hold a grudge.

When the backlash finally arrived, at the end of last year, it seemed like a letdown. No one can deny that Eminem's race has a lot to do with his huge popularity, and it might have been exciting to hear, say, Jay-Z or Nas say so. Instead, we got clumsy dis tracks from B-team rapper Benzino, character assassination from Benzino's magazine, *The Source*, and more clumsy dis tracks, from Ja Rule, who growled, "You'll never know black pain/But you could become the first white rapper slain." On G-Unit's "Bump Heads," Eminem offered playful taunts in response: "Just keep singing that same song recycled/We'd all much rather get along than fight you/Me and Hailie dance to your songs/We like you." It was like listening to an outtake from *8 Mile*.

For years now, Eminem has been predicting not just his own downfall but his own obsolescence, a byproduct of popularity. On "Without Me," he imitated an imagination-deprived record executive: "Hey! Here's a concept that works/Twenty million other white rappers emerge." But the imitators never showed up. Eminem is bigger than Kurt Cobain ever was, so you would think he'd be just as influential, but he has yet to attract an army of sound-alikes, the way Cobain did. (The answer may have something to do with the fact that hip-hop is harder to master than grunge.) There is no movement, no trend; there's just him, bigger and more isolated than ever.

In some ways, isolation suits Eminem. He has never seemed totally comfortable trading lame punch lines with D12, and although Shady Records has scored a huge hit with 50 Cent, he and Eminem seem to see each other more as business partners than as collaborators. The two performed together at the Summer Jam X concert in Giants Stadium in June, and although they presented a united front onstage, the audience reaction wasn't quite so unanimous. Maybe it was the rain or the lineup or just the night, but by the time Eminem took the stage for his headlining spot, many of the black attendees had split, and the crowd that stuck around looked a lot like the "White America" Eminem raps about. But "White America" wouldn't have meant as much if it had been delivered by, say, Good Charlotte—a white rock band with white fans. When Eminem raps his version, the true target seems to be not White America but non-White America; he's telling black rap fans that he knows what they're thinking and that he cares what they think. Eminem is always bragging about challenging his listeners, but it seems that these are the only listeners who really challenge him. And you can't help but wonder what he'll do when there's no one left who's willing to put up a fight.

POP MUSIC'S WAR OF WORDS

by Jon Pareles

from the *New York Times*,
February 18, 2001

In the furor that has surrounded this year's Grammy contenders for Album of the Year, it may surprise no one to hear that one of the nominated albums includes a song whose narrator gloats over his affair with an underage girl and tries to pressure her into a threesome. Or that another tune from the album is about a man propositioning his young cousin.

But those songs don't come from Eminem's widely denounced "The Marshall Mathers LP," which has been attacked by groups that consider it misogynistic and homophobic. Actually, "Janie Runaway" and "Cousin Dupree" are two of the catchier songs on Steely Dan's "Two Against Nature." While some Grammy-watchers expect Paul Simon's "You're the One" to win the award on Wednesday, others are

NOISE

predicting that "Two Against Nature" will be the album that voters in the National Academy of Recording Arts and Sciences will rally around to fight off Eminem's barbarism, especially since Steely Dan never got a Grammy in its 1970's heyday (Radiohead's "Kid A" and Beck's "Midnite Vultures" are also nominated.)

Steely Dan's songwriters, Walter Becker and Donald Fagen, get a free pass from the watchdogs of content because it's understood that they are, like most artists, professional liars, otherwise known as storytellers. Mr. Becker and Mr. Fagen, like many novelists, screenwriters and playwrights, create sleazeballs and empathize enough to make them believable. That means capturing cousin Dupree's longing for "a down-home family romance" and sketching the thought process when the narrator of "Janie Runaway" considers a country getaway to Pennsylvania, then reconsiders crossing state lines: "Or would that be a federal case?"

It's widely accepted that "Janie Runaway" doesn't mean Steely Dan endorses statutory rape. Mr. Becker and Mr. Fagen happen to be curious about how their character would coax his "wonderwaif," about his rationalizations and self-delusions, about the ways a conscience can warp to accept repulsive actions. They also like the perverse frisson of wrapping a creepy monologue in highbrow chord changes and luxuriously nonchalant arrangements.

Steely Dan's music isn't abrasive like hip-hop. It's at the opposite extreme, cool and enticing. Some listeners might even find themselves singing along with deeply unsavory come-ons. The group's audience, mostly boomer-age adults, considers itself sophisticated enough to handle a few ironies and the concept of an unreliable narrator, and the music goes down so smoothly that it seems perfectly genteel. Mr. Becker and Mr. Fagen are punctilious pop craftsmen who have spent a long time in the music business. So Steely Dan is granted literary license. Similarly, there was no controversy when Shawn Colvin's "Sunny Came Home"—about a woman who takes revenge on an abusive husband by burning down the house—received Grammys as Record of the Year and Song of the Year for 1997, even if it was pro-arson.

Eminem gets no such leeway. He's belligerent, foul-mouthed and sick-minded, and his favorite all-purpose insult is a homophobic slur. (In a defense that's both weak and disagreeable, he has said he doesn't mean it to apply only to homosexuals.) Where Steely Dan uses insinuation and indirection, Eminem is bluntly antagonistic; where Steely Dan lives for understatement, Eminem goes for hyperbole.

Instead of the Slim Shady alias he used on his previous album (which, incidentally, won two Grammy awards for "rap" without any repercussions), Eminem uses his real name in the title of "The Marshall Mathers LP." And his music is hip-hop, which renders him immediately suspect to much of the baby-boom generation. Somehow, all those factors make him forfeit the presumption that every word on his album is not completely, unironically sincere. He'd be the first artist who, to paraphrase Philip Roth, never made anything up.

And if that were so, he'd probably be safely behind bars. Between the murders, death threats, rapes, bank robbery, drug abuse, drunken driving, fistfighting, vandalism, animal mutilation and the notion that, as he sarcastically raps, "I invented violence," Eminem would be a full-time crime wave. Op-ed handwringers, who are used to parsing the straight-faced pronouncements of politicians, can glean all the scurrilous quotes they need. People who worry about domestic abuse (most of Eminem's misogyny is directed at his wife and his mother) and about homophobia also have plenty of ammunition. All of them help Eminem reach his true objective: "I think I was put here to annoy the world."

Where Steely Dan plays one basic identity game—imper-

JON PARELES

sonating louse after louse—Mr. Mathers runs a multiple-identity Olympics. He's a success, a loser, a madman, a star, a whiner, a combatant, a jerk—anything, he insists, but a hypocrite. He portrays realistic irritation spilling over into homicidal rampages, and as a child of the tabloids, he exploits his own troubled real-life marriage, like Henny Youngman turned bloodthirsty. He knows he's a mess; he also jeers that plenty of other people have thoughts like his that they're unwilling to admit. "Yeah, I probably got a couple of screws up in my head loose," he raps. "But no worse than what's goin' on in your parents' bedrooms."

Unlike many of his detractors, Eminem regularly makes a distinction between words and action. In "Stan," in which a deranged fan tries to impress Eminem by acting out the mayhem in his songs, Eminem can't believe that Stan didn't know that what he said was "just clownin'." In "Who Knew," Eminem insists, "I just said it, I ain't know if you'd do it or not." In "The Way I Am," he explains that blurting out berserk fantasies "helps in itself to relieve all this tension dispensin' these sentences."

Meanwhile, the music connotes comedy: bouncy keyboard lines, whiz-crunch sound effects. Eminem leaves it to listeners to separate his Grand Guignol humor from his position statements, and so far, the fans may be better literary analysts than the horrified adults. While fans laugh at Eminem and root for his general defiance, deranged copycats like Stan are just figments of Eminem's imagination.

Eminem knows full well that notoriety means sales. The more censure is heaped on him, the more respect he gains from disaffected teenagers. What may be the funniest part of the Grammy hoopla is that Eminem-haters think the imprimatur of the Grammy would be to Eminem's advantage.

If "The Marshall Mathers LP" were named Album of the Year, they seem to think, Eminem would be established in the pop mainstream, with his four-letter words and vicious fantasies certified as acceptable behavior. Why, he'd be up there in the Grammy pantheon with Album of the Year winners like Celine Dion, Tony Bennett, Eric Clapton, Natalie Cole and Santana, respectable as all get-out.

In a conspiratorial universe, it's conceivable, barely, that the Grammy Awards have learned some perverse strategies from the likes of Steely Dan. Irony-poor protests aimed at Eminem's nomination may have failed to appreciate what could be a brilliant bit of pop-culture jujitsu. Giving Eminem the award, or even letting him get near it, just might certify him as one more piece of popcraft, a show-business act who doesn't even scare the graybeards at the Grammys. He can thrive as a scourge and an underdog, but Grammy approval could torpedo his credibility in an instant.

NOISE

THE ANGRY APPEAL OF EMINEM IS CUTTING ACROSS RACIAL LINES

by Lynette Holloway

from the *New York Times*,
October 28, 2002

the Bronx River Houses are hallowed ground in the hip-hop world, one of the neighborhoods where young African-Americans and Hispanics helped create a new art form in the 1970's. The housing project in the South Bronx takes its heritage seriously. From there emerged a founder of hip-hop, Afrika Bambaataa, and the loose-knit group of D.J.'s, dancers, graffiti artists and rappers called Zulu Nation.

Three decades later, the No. 1 selling rapper in the country is a 30-year-old white man, Eminem, born Marshall Bruce Mathers III. Only three years ago, he was derided as "the Elvis of hip-hop," or a raw version of the 1980's flattopped performer Vanilla Ice (no comparison could be worse on these streets). But these days at "the Bricks," as the Bronx River

Houses are called, there is no resentment, there are no complaints about Eminem's racial identity.

Not only is Eminem accepted as a supremely skillful practitioner of rap, many say he is the salvation of an art form that they say has been corrupted by a focus on Bentleys, yachts and Cristal Champagne.

"You don't see him wearing thousand-pound gold chains encrusted with ice," Manaury Reyes, 17, said of Eminem. "He's always dressed regular in sweats like us. The sweats might cost more, but he ain't frontin'. He's not rapping about clothes, cars and jewelry like all those other rappers. He's rapping about life—you know, stuff that we go through out here. Some of it's a goof, but some of it's real, and it sounds like it comes from the heart, you know. A lot of us can relate to that."

This is the kind of loyalty that executives at Universal Pictures, which is owned by Vivendi Universal, are counting on when "8 Mile," starring Eminem, is released on Nov. 8. The film, loosely based on Eminem's life, is the latest test of the rapper's crossover appeal. The film's title refers to the rough-and-tumble neighborhood that is Detroit's racial and economic divide.

While it is well known among music industry executives that hip-hop consumers are more than 75 percent nonblack (Eminem's core audience is suburban white teenagers), Universal Pictures will need to reach into minority audiences to make "8 Mile" a hit.

Hip-hop artists are a proven box-office draw. "Barbershop," an urban comedy starring Ice Cube, grossed an estimated $69.5 million by Saturday since its release on Sept. 13. "Brown Sugar," a hip-hop love story starring Taye Diggs, grossed $22.4 million since its release on Oct. 11. Last year, "Exit Wounds," starring DMX, grossed $52 million. The main artists in these movies have been black. But no one expects

Eminem's race will keep blacks and Hispanics from going to the box office.

"Eminem gets a pass in the same vein that back during segregation black folks had to be better than average, had to be the best, to be accepted," said Stephen Hill, vice president for music and talent at Black Entertainment Television. "Eminem is better than the best. In his own way, he is the best lyricist, alliterator and enunciator out there in hip-hop music. In terms of rapping about the pain that other disenfranchised people feel, there is no one better at their game than Eminem."

There are some skeptics. Star, a host of an often raunchy, racially frank radio program, "Star and Buc Wild Morning Show" on WQHT-FM in New York, said that Eminem may be the world's best rapper, but that he benefits from institutional racism.

"Big deals aren't given to the black producers or artists," he said. "They are given to the white kids, the people that the executives feel comfortable with."

In the end, even skeptics give Eminem credit. Star pointed out that Eminem has earned credibility in the black community because he does not run from the "Elvis thing."

Eminem jokes about it. On the track, "White America," on the album, "The Eminem Show," he says, "Let's do the math—if I was black, I would've sold half," he said explaining why a white rapper sells more albums than black rappers.

And he does sell albums. He is one of the few bright spots in a music industry suffering from declining CD sales. His latest album, "The Eminem Show," has sold 6.7 million copies domestically, more than any other rapper has in any one year, according to Nielsen SoundScan, which has been tracking such sales since 1991.

This year, Eminem has outsold some of the most popular hip-hop artists, all of them black. Nelly has sold 4.2 million copies; Ludacris, 2 million; and Ja Rule, 1.6 million, according to Nielsen SoundScan.

The strategic early release of "Lose Yourself," a single from the "8 Mile" soundtrack, has not hurt. It was No. 2 last week in Billboard's Top 10 singles charts.

On a windswept basketball court at the cluster of neatly kept brown-brick projects at 174th Street and Stratford Avenue, teenagers gave Eminem credit for "keeping it real." They see him both as a rebel rising up against a brutal parent and as the devoted father they never had. Throughout his album, "The Eminem Show," he pledges to his daughter, Hailie Jade, 6, everlasting love and support.

The album boldly recounts the rapper's depressing childhood, though it is difficult to tell fact from fiction. He raps about his hatred of his mother, Debbie Mathers-Briggs (whom he says was a drug addict and who unsuccessfully sued him for slander), his ex-wife Kim Mathers, and the news media.

To the teenagers at the Bricks, Eminem's life, as he tells it, was harsher than their own—that which they cared to reveal. Many grew up in homes supported by single mothers. They say it is unfathomable that a mother would treat a child anything like Eminem describes in his song, "Cleanin' Out My Closet."

In the song, he asks his mother, "Remember when Ronnie died, and you wished it was me?" (Ronnie Polkingharn was an uncle who committed suicide.) Then, he continues, with words aimed to strike at any mother's heart: "Hailie's getting so big now. You should see her, she's beautiful. But you'll never see her. She won't even be at your funeral."

Andre Hannah, 14, said: "My dads is gone. It would be cool if my dad was there for me like he's there for his daughter. I mean, he loves her more than he loves his wife and mother."

Teenagers love that Eminem challenges elected officials, whose attacks on the singer only cement their loyalty to him.

Last summer, he named his concert tour, the Anger Management Tour. It mockingly featured sound bites from Congressional hearings and newscasts describing him as vulgar, degenerate, homophobic, antisocial, misogynistic and "noise and mind pollution." He did not disagree.

Teenagers appreciate Eminem's respect for his producer and mentor, Dr. Dre, who is black and helped give him credibility in the hip-hop world.

"When I first saw Eminem, I thought he wasn't going to last," said Charles Rosario, 15, a student at Christopher Columbus High School in the South Bronx. "I thought he was going to be another phony like Vanilla Ice.

"He came out with that song, 'My Name Is,' " he said. "I was like, 'Oh, man. Who is this fake?' But Dr. Dre gave it some nice beats and stuff."

Jose Gallardeo, 16, a student at James Monroe High School in the South Bronx, says that Eminem's revenge fantasies, which have included raping his mother and killing his ex-wife, give him an edge over other rappers.

"It's the kind of music that makes you stop and say, 'Is this dude for real?' " he said. "He's not like everybody else."

Mike Brisbain, 18, who lives in the Bronx River Houses, is unimpressed: "He needs to calm down with all that crazy white-boy stuff—that fight music, yo. That's gonna get him hurt. He's a good lyricist. He should concentrate on that."

Davon Pleasant, 15, a student at Lewis and Clark High School, was the lone detractor. He prefers DMX, the raspy-voiced hardcore rapper from Yonkers.

"I don't like him," he said of Eminem. "He talks about killing his wife in his songs. I don't care what she did to him. That's wrong."

LYNETTE HOLLOWAY

THE PRESIDENT'S FRIEND

by Johann Hari

from *The Independent*,
January 12, 2003

elvis Presley, James Dean, Johnny Rotten . . . Eminem. Every generation has its iconic rebel, and the Noughties' symbol of mummy-scaring and daddy-aggravating rebellion will be in our faces even more than usual over the next few weeks. Not only is his first movie, *8 Mile*, hitting our screens, but hip-hop (Eminem's musical domain) stands accused by the Home Secretary, David Blunkett, of contributing to Britain's burgeoning gun culture. So who is this strange 28-year-old who is whipping up everyone from Lynne Cheney (wife of Dick, the US Vice-President), who called him "despicable", to Kim Howells, our own Culture Minister? And is he really such a threat?

The basic biographical details of Marshall Mathers III (the

moniker "Eminem" is based on his initials) are familiar to anybody who has heard his music or seen his movie. For better or worse, his claim to be the authentic voice of dispossessed, white, working-class American men is lent credence by the dull predictability of his early life. His now notorious mother, Debbie, married his father when she was 15, and his father disappeared when Eminem was six months old, only to resurface more than 20 years later when his son was a multimillionaire. The rapper explained that he would rather "slit my dad's throat" than meet him.

Eminem was bitter about being abandoned to what he calls "a stereotypical white-trash, trailer-park upbringing" in the mostly black neighbourhoods of east Detroit, where he was regularly beaten by the other kids—once so badly that he suffered a cerebral haemorrhage and was in a coma for 10 days. Meanwhile, he would try to protect his younger brother, Nate, from what he alleges were his mother's excessive drinking and drug use.

The barely fictionalised 8 Mile, which feels like a strange mix of TV mini-series biopic and Shakespearean verse drama, picks up the story of his teenage years—or, at least, Eminem's version of them. He dropped out of school in ninth grade ("I don't think it's necessarily 'cos I'm stupid," he has said. "I just didn't go to school. I couldn't deal . . . ") and threw himself into Detroit's local rap scene. As a white boy, he was viewed with suspicion—as one black rival tells him in the movie, "This is hip-hop. You're a tourist."

When Eminem walked on stage during rap "battles"— staged competitions in down-town clubs—he would get booed so loudly that at first he couldn't even get heard. "But when the motherfuckers heard my rhymes," he says, "they shut the fuck up."

After years honing his craft in Detroit, Eminem came second in the rap Olympics—and a tape of his sounds made its way to Dr Dre, founder of the seminal group NWA (Niggaz

With Attitude). Eminem became, within a few years, hip-hop's breakthrough into the ultra-mainstream. As a white man, some critics have claimed, Eminem was able to take the genre into places that racism had previously excluded it from, a latterday "minstrel" misappropriating black music — that's just one of the tornado-like controversies that quickly surrounded the rapper.

Within a few years of super-stardom, he was being sued by his mother and grandmother for "grossly misrepresenting" them in his music, and his wife for singing about murdering her and for encouraging audiences at his concerts to rip apart inflated dolls bearing her name; he was being damned in the US Congress for "corrupting America's youth"; and he was being claimed by right-wing voices as a symbol of all that is great about America.

Yes, you read that last one right. Since the release of 8 Mile, there has been a shift in perceptions of Eminem that would leave the collective minds of Nostradamus and Mystic Meg boggling. Listen, for example, to US conservative pundit Gerry Marzorati: "The Eminem story — or the movie version that unfolded in 8 Mile — is an echt [genuine] Republican story, one about pulling yourself up and overcoming your circumstances while your pathetic single mom waits around for a handout ... So, does Eminem get to do the Super Bowl half-time show [the pinnacle of mainstream Middle American entertainment]? I mean, what's left besides a White House drop-by? Which might not be all that far-fetched, given the warmth of the mainstream's embrace of Mr Mathers. There are precedents: gun-toting Elvis's visit with Nixon, Michael Jackson's photo op with Reagan." Eminem and Dubya, posing side-by-side? Both are fervently pro-gun: Eminem celebrates gun culture on every album, while Dubya is fervently backed by the National Rifle Association and even passed a law as Governor of Texas which permitted the carrying of concealed weapons in church.

Right-wing journalist Andrew Sullivan, who is close to the Bush administration, thinks the two could be soul mates in other ways too, explaining, "I too was struck by the ferocious individualism of the movie, 8 *Mile*. Yes, his friends were crucial. But the message of the story was that you have to escape from hell by yourself. Any other way is somehow inauthentic. And that rough independence is another reason why I find Eminem so appealing and intoxicating."

At first, Bush's self-righteous moral conservatism seems hard to reconcile with the more full-on Eminem lyrics. In "Amityville", he raps: "My little sister's birthday, she'll remember me/ For a gift I had ten of my boys take her virginity/ And bitches know me as a horny-ass freak/ Their mother wasn't raped, I ate her pussy while she was 'sleep." Not likely to be the 2004 Bush presidential campaign tune, I suspect. Yet 8 *Mile* does reveal something fundamentally right-wing about the Eminem phenomenon: although he challenges Middle America's sensibilities with his swearing and shock tactics, ultimately he reinforces their value system and the extent to which they see their privileged economic status as legitimate.

The two key pillars of privileged American society—the market and the sanctity of the family unit—are at the core of Eminem's vision. The fact that Eminem and his younger brother (depicted in the movie, presumably so that even more of his relatives don't sue, as a little sister) spent their childhoods shunting from trailer park to trailer park and often went hungry is not attributed in the film to a culture which tolerates massive inequality and a welfare system which guarantees that child poverty will exist. The one character in 8 *Mile* who does attempt this kind of social analysis, a Nation of Islam supporter, is presented as absurd, a joke figure.

No, all of Eminem's failings are blamed on the moral inadequacy of his mother. She is depicted as lazy—"Get a fucking job," he snaps at her, adopting the tone of Saffy from

Absolutely Fabulous—undisciplined, and, worst of all, interested in her own sexual fulfilment.

Indeed, everyone in the ghetto is seen as somehow morally lax compared to Eminem, who, through sheer dint of his commitment to the market and hard work, will lift himself out of poverty while the others deservedly remain there.

And 8 *Mile* also appeals to thinkers like Sullivan because it is a story of "anti-white racism"—a phenomenon which the US right has latched on to with glee. David Horowitz, one of the US's leading neoconservative thinkers, has written a book entitled Hating Whitey and Other Progressive Causes. They claim that racism cuts both ways, and discriminates against both whites like Eminem and against black people.

This is, of course, true to a very limited extent, but Horowitz and others use the Eminem story as a way to assert moral equivalence between the two. The beating of Rodney King by white Los Angeles police officers is, they imply, not really any worse than Eminem being booed off stage by black people; blacks cannot claim to be victims of racism in America because everybody is. This, of course, is absurd: whites were not enslaved, they do not make up the vast majority of the prison population and the victims of the death penalty, and they are overwhelmingly more powerful. But the Eminem story implies otherwise: Eminem is white man as victim of black prejudice.

Eminem also plays to the right's opposition to feminism. Sketching another parallel with Dubya, Richard Goldstein, executive editor of *The Village Voice*, explains, "Both draw their power from the compelling image of the strong man posing as the common man. Both played the populist card to win the nation's heart. And I would argue that both owe their success to the sexual backlash . . . [They are guilty of] nostalgia for a world where male power seems righteous, especially when it's allied with the truth-telling vitality of the street.

"*8 Mile* is a feel-good movie with precisely that scenario . . . Class trumps race, while repressing the real reason why black and white men can bond over a rapper like Eminem: he gives them a common enemy—women."

This can be heard again and again in his lyrics, and especially in the celebration of violence against women. Slim Shady, a character Eminem has adopted as his "evil" alter ago, raps, "My life's like kind of what my wife's like—fucked up after I beat her fucking ass every night." Or how about: "I don't give a fuck, if this chick was my own mother, I'd still fuck her with no rubber, and cum inside her." The rapper claims that nobody would take this seriously, that he is only playing a role, but the sight of hundreds of testosterone-soaked men rapping along to this—something I've witnessed—gives the opposite impression.

Eminem's music is saturated with the sense that women have become too assertive, too powerful. Eminem traces his own feeling of disempowerment again and again to women— either his "slut" (ie sexually active) mother, his ex-wife, or women generally. Rape serves in his raps as his way of reasserting control over "mouthy" women. He has even mooted starring in a porn film where he "fucks all the women who have ever dissed me"—silencing those "bitches" who should have known their place.

So, yes, Eminem is an icon of rebellion. But where Elvis rebelled against the sexually puritan strand of 1950s America, James Dean against the refusal to take the emotional life of teenagers (especially gay ones) seriously, and Johnny Rotten against established power in all its forms, Eminem is a symptom of the backlash against all this. He is spearheading a rebellion against the progress charted by earlier youth icons. A generation of Eminem fans is not quite, I imagine, what the Sixties generation expected to give birth to.

permissions

"Eminem's Dirty Secrets" by M.L. Elrick. Copyright © 2000 by M.L. Erick and Detroit Free Press. Reprinted by permission of the author.

"8 Mile" by William Bowers. Copyright © 2003 by William Bowers. Reprinted by permission of the author. Originally appeared at www.pitchforkmedia.com, January 21, 2003.

"Moral Abdication or Just Father-Son Bonding with a Creepy Edge" by Mark Cochrane. Copyright © 2003 by Pacific Newspaper Group, Inc. Material reprinted with the express permission of Pacific Newspaper Group Inc., a CanWest Partnership. Originally appeared in *The Vancouver Sun*, February 22, 2003.

"The Boy on the Bus" by Craig Taylor. Copyright © 2000 by Craig Taylor. Reprinted by permission of the author. Originally appeared at www.openletters.net, July 18, 2000.

"He Can't Keep Saying the Same Shit" by Alexis Petridis and Giles Foden. Copyright © 2002 by The Guardian. Reprinted by permission. Originally appeared in *The Guardian*, May 24, 2002.

"Eminem's Martyr Complex" by Gerald Marzorati. Copyright © 2002 by Gerald Marzorati. Reprinted by permission of the author. Originally appeared at www.slate.com, May 30, 2002.

"White American" by Robert Christgau. Copyright © 2002 by Robert Christgau. Reprinted with permission of the author. Originally appeared in *The Village Voice*, June 11, 2002.

"The Eminem Shtick" by Richard Goldstein. Copyright © 2002 by Richard Goldstein. Reprinted by permission of the author. Originally appeared in the *Village Voice*, June 18, 2002.

"Guess Who Thinks Eminem's a Genius? Middle-Aged Me" by Paul Slansky. Copyright © 2002 by Paul Slansky. Reprinted by permission of the author. Originally appeared in The New York Observer, June 3, 2002.

"Sympathy for the Devil" by Kelefa Sanneh. Copyright © by Kelefa Sanneh. Reprinted by permission of the author. Originally appeared in *The New Yorker*, June 24, 2002.

"But Can He Act?" by Geoff Boucher. Copyright © 2002 by The Los Angeles Times. Reprinted with permission. Originally appeared in The *Los Angeles Times*, October 13, 2002.

"White Hot: From Rap to Riches" by Elvis Mitchell. Copyright © 2002 by The New York Times Co. Reprinted with permission. Originally appeared in *The New York Times*, November 8, 2002.

"Mr. Ambassador" by Frank Rich. Copyright © 2002 by The New York Times Co. Reprinted with permission. Originally appeared in *The New York Times*, November 3, 2002.

"White Man's Burden" by Roy Grundmann. Copyright © 2003 by Cineaste. Reprinted with permission. Originally appeared in *Cineaste*, Spring 2003.

"The Eminem Consensus" by Richard Goldstein. Copyright © 2002 by Richard Goldstein. Reprinted by permission of the author. Originally appeared in the *Village Voice*, November 19, 2002.

"Crossover Dream" by R.J. Smith. Copyright © 2002 by R.J. Smith. Reprinted by permission of the author. Originally appeared in the *Village Voice*, November 6-12, 2002.

"What Eminem Means and Doesn't" by Robert Christgau. Copyright © 2002 by Robert Christgau. Reprinted with permission of the author. Originally appeared in *The Los Angeles Times*.

"Eminem—Bad Rap?" by Richard Kim. Copyright © 2001 by Richard Kim. Reprinted by permission of the author. Originally appeared in *The Nation*, March 5, 2001.

"The Kids are Alright" by Hank Stuever. Copyright © 2001 by The Washington Post Writers Group. Reprinted by permission. Originally appeared in *The Washington Post*, February 28, 2001.

"Why Eminem Should Get the Grammy" by Whet Moser. Copyright © 2001 by Whet Moser. Reprinted by permission of the author. Originally appeared at Salon.,com, February 21, 2001.

"Genius-Not!" by Armond White. Copyright © 2003 by Armond White. Reprinted by permission of the author. Originally appeared at firstofthemonth.org.

"Voice of America" by Kelefa Sanneh. Copyright © 2003 by Kelefa Sanneh. Reprinted by permission of the author. Originally appeared in *Rolling Stone*, June 24, 2002.

"Pop Music's War of Words" by Jon Pareles. Copyright © 2001 by The New York Times Co. Reprinted with permission. Originally appeared in *The New York Times*, February 18, 2001.

"The Angry Appeal of Eminem" by Lynette Holloway. Copyright © 2002 by The New York Times Co. Reprinted with permission. Originally appeared in *The New York Times*, October 30, 2002.

"The President's Friend" by Johann Hari. Copyright © 2003 by The Independent. Reprinted by permission. Originally appeared in *The Independent*, January 12, 2003.

Photo Permissions

Eminem arrives in Westwood Village for the world premiere of the film "8 Mile" November 6, 2002 in Los Angeles. Copyright © Reuters NewMedia Inc./CORBIS. Reprinted with permission.

Eminem holds his Video Music Award , September, 07 2000 in New York. Copyright © AFP/CORBIS. Reprinted with permission.

Eminem performs at the MTV Video Music Awards 29 August, 2002 in New York. Copyright © AFP/CORBIS. Reprinted with permission.

Marshall Bruce Mathers, better known as rapper Eminem pleads guilty to carrying a concealed weapon in probate Judge Antonio Viviano courtroom in Macomb County Circuit Judge on 14 February 2001 in Mount Clemens, Michigan. Copyright © AFP/CORBIS. Reprinted with permission.

The rapper, whose lyrics have shocked parents and human rights activists across the world, makes his entrance wielding a chainsaw and wearing an ice-hockey mask. Copyright © HELLESTAD RUNE/CORBIS SYGMA. Reprinted with permission.

Eminem holds baby doll out of window. Copyright © Newsquest, Ltd (The Herald). Reprinted by permission. Reprinted with permission.

Eminem tosses baby doll in air. Copyright © Newsquest, Ltd (The Herald). Reprinted by permission. Reprinted with permission.

Eminem gives a cameraman the finger as he enters the Source Hip-Hop Awards: Eminem attends the "Source Hip-Hop Awards", Hollywood, California, August 18, 1999. (Photo by Brenda Chase / Online USA / Liaison Agency). Credit: Getty Images. Reprinted with permission.

Eminem on stage with blow-up doll: Eminem performs at "Dreamcast presents the Nike ACG Indoor," America's first indoor snowboard quarterpipe competition and music festival held at the Great Western Forum, Sat., Sept. 9th. Photo by Kevin Winter/Getty Images. Credit: Getty Images. Reprinted with permission.

Elton John and Eminem perform at the 43rd Annual Grammy Awards at Staples Center, Los Angeles, Ca. 2/21/01. (Photo by Kevin Winter/Getty Images). Credit: Getty Images. Reprinted with permission.

An Eminem doll featuring a chain saw, manufactured by Art Asylum, is set to be released this year. The lifelike doll has the rapper's tattoos recreated in detail, including the words "Cut Here" on his neck. Eminem, who has a huge hit with the song "The Real Slim Shady," caused a storm by waving a chain saw on stage during his recent tour. (Photo by Art Asylum/Courtesy of Getty Images). Credit: Getty Images. Reprinted with permission.

Eminem presents MTV Video Music Award with puppet from Comedy Central's Crank Yankers: NEW YORK - AUGUST 28: (U.S. TABLOIDS OUT) Singer Eminem speaks onstage during the 2003 MTV Video Music Awards at Radio City Music Hall on August 28, 2003 in New York City. (Photo by Scott Gries/Getty Images). Credit: Getty Images. Reprinted with permission.